Anahita Huber
Goldsentences and Miraclewords

Dedicated to my daughter and two sons
Marianne Desiree, Beat Simon and Boris Alex
who I love dearly
and who I would have loved to have treated in the way I now teach to other parents! Thank you for being the most wonderful experience and teachers in my life.
Thank you for being.

And to all parents, teachers and caring-persons
who would like to change things in parenting, education and child-care because they know:

educating is relating

Original Version in German "Zauberwörter und Goldsätze"
April 2017
English Version „Goldsentences and Miraclewords"
December 2017

Why This Book? Or Better: What For?

After making my first experiences in applying the integrative method of Mària Kenessey (Institute for integrative Psychology and Pedagogics IfiPP) and writing about them in and publishing the first two books about the integrative pedagogy in primary-music-school and music-school, both in German language, in the last years more and more the wish arouse to collect and summarise the 'goldsentences and miraclewords' which make parenting so much more easy into a small manual. Some friends wished to have such a practical companion in their pockets ready to use, on the way, on the playground, on the train, in the restaurant, or visiting friends and so on. And then, when I visited Goa in January 2017 they asked: can`t you translate this into English? Okay, I did it!!!

So – here it is! Take it as a working-book, doing your exercises, write into it, take notes and make supplements.

It was really wonderful and great fun for me to collect the numerous themes, to pick up uncounted situations and write the useful sentences to accompany them. Ahead of all you can find a short introduction as well as some explanations so that people who have never heard of this method can learn what`s it all about. This booklet is a practical supplement to my other two books of integrative education or parenting (see at the back) and to Mària Kenessey`s book „The integrative Parenting-basic-training" in German, Spanish, Hungarian and Serbian. To her I owe this huge treasure and wealth of actually simple and so precious knowledge. It has been sleeping inside me and was awakened, remembered, refined and extended through the study at the IfiPP over several years. I have been passing it on and am teaching it now since 2001 for over fifteen years with a lot of pleasure and joy – not only to parents but to all people who work or are with children and who want to simplify dealing with difficult situations or to ease the parenting-every-day-life, to improve the family-climate and reinforce the relationship to the child. Some of them already realized in the parenting-basic-training that we can use the constructive communication for example also with the partner and actually with all people, the language adjusted to the age. And remember when you find it not so easy, to encourage yourself with one of the rhymes of my songs (sorry, except this one all in German: „Hejo, together we are strong, helping each other as we go along, together we shall make it, together we shall make it!")

„**We are still practicing and learn more every day.**
For today we are good enough, we`re getting better
(... all the time, as the Beatles sing - haha!)
A lot of patience with yourself, joy and success!
Let`s get closer – not only me to you and you to me and your children but most of all you to yourself. Because this is a big and an important step in accompaning children.

> **When we sense ourselves we realise and feel**
> **better and better what`s going on in children.**
> A.H.

> **Encouragement is the most important element**
> **in child-upbringing.**
> (Rudolf Dreikurs)

Healthy self-esteem:
"I can butter my croissant all alone!"
Nepomuk, 2 ½ years old

Anahita Huber

Goldsentences and Miraclewords

Of the Integrative Treasure-Box

For a More Relaxed Everyday-Life With Kids

Contents

Language is the Most Important Medium in Bringing up Children ... 11

Dumping Space For the 'Present Day' Language ... 14

We Always Take Our Own Education With Us ... 18

Constructive Communication
 – The 'Yes-Language' ... 21

The Acknowledgement of Brain-Research ... 29

The Integrative Dealing with Feelings ... 33

The Four Erroneous Goals of the Child According to Mària Kenessey and Rudolf Dreikurs ... 39

Summary – What We Can Do, How We Can Optimise Our Relationships ... 45

List of Miracle Words ... 48

Concrete Examples
In The Use of 'Golden Sentences', Themes ... 50

What Means Integrative Parenting? ... 197
The Kenessey-Method ... 198
The Children`s Rights UNICEF ... 199

Anahita Huber –Biography ... 202
Contact and Information ... 202
Integrative Pedagogy Books by Anahita Huber ... 203
Thanks ... 204

Concrete Examples in the Use of 'Golden Sentences' ; Issues and Themes

Aggression:
  Biting, Scratching, Hitting, Pushing and Screaming ... 52
Arriving Late ... 190
Attention ... 68
Autonomy (Getting Dressed) ... 59
Bed-Wetting ... 77
Being Quiet ... 135
Brushing Teeth ... 185
Changing Nappies ... 182
Class-Rules by Class-Council ... 160
Conflict and Reconciliation ... 159
Death ... 170
Demanding, Overstraining, Patronising or Promoting ... 100
Disturbing ... 148
Dry and Clean: Nappies, Potty, WC, Washing ys. ... 131
Encouragement ... 85
Family Council ... 63
Fear ... 58
Feelings,
  Emotions (Anger, Rage, Fear, Joy, Sadness) ... 103
Fighting Back, Defending (Yourself) ... 181
Food, Meals and Table-Manners ... 88
Getting Dressed (Autonomy) ... 59
Getting Up in the Morning ... 71
Going Shopping ... 81
Good-Bye, Farewell, Cutting the Umbilical Cord ... 50
Helping ... 109
Homework ... 107
Illness ... 116
Jealousy (Fear of Loss) ... 79
Limits ... 105
Listening ... 189

Lying ... 118
Making a Call ... 170 (see 'Being Quiet' ... 135)
Media (TV, Mobiles, Computer) ... 120
Misbehaviour ... 93, ... 96, 178
Needs ... 73
Neglecting Misbehaviour ... 93, ... 96, ... 178
Orders, Commands ... 75
Pacifier / Dummy, Crying and Comforting ... 125
Play 'Boss' ... 78
Pocket-Money ... 167
Praising ... 66, ... 111
Quarrelling (Between Siblings) ... 153
Resistance ... 183
Role Model ... 180
Rules ... 130
Sadness, Grief ... 172
Saying Sorry ... 82
School-age: Class-Rules ... 160,
  Conflict and Reconciliation ... 159, Disturbing ... 148,
  Class-Council ... 162
Sharing, Taking Away ... 167
Swearing, Being Cheeky (Impudent) ... 97
Sweets, Candy and Chewing-Gum ... 122
Sexuality ... 140
Sleeping ... 137
Stealing ... 144
Tantrums and Fits:
  About the so-called 'Tantrum-Phase' ... 174
Tasks, Jobs, Responsibilities, Family-Council ... 63
Telling Tales, Complaining ... 114

I decided with Susan R., my proof-reader, to use the English version of words in this book. Like centre, colour, behaviour etc.
Sometimes you might find a 'weird expression'. Then it might be that I wanted it like that as part of the 'new language'. Enjoy!

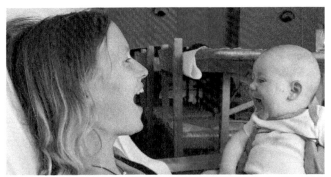
Yasha with Aaliyah in mutual enthusiastic communication

Language is the Most Important Medium in Bringing up Children

Why?
Because we communicate mostly with it and therefore we can reach each other in this way. Everything we say changes the feelings of human beings we talk to as well as the whole surrounding.

When we understand constructive communication (coco) and use the right sentences and words we can save ourselves and the children much sorrow, pain and anger. The advantage is that children are much easier to cope with, to be with and to bring up. Living and being together becomes easier and more relaxed when we know and use these words and sentences and remember to use the right tone. When we do we don`t have to 'educate' so much anymore.

The tone makes the music.

The attitude behind our communication also plays an important role.

When I`m angry I can hardly say a friendly word. Then I am forced to deal with my own anger first before I communicate my request.

**When I am angry I take a pause in parenting.
For the child`s sake and my own.**

To communicate constructively means to reach the 'joy-centre' in the brain (the self-rewarding centre) where the beloved feel-good-hormone Dopamine is produced.

Joy, acknowledgement, appreciation, success, the feeling of well-being and belonging releases this hormone. The consequence is that the children will find it easier to cooperate using their own free will and making their own decisions. Power-struggles no longer take place   (and if they do, we know how to side step them or to step out of them) so that everything runs smoother, more efficiently and with more joy. When the important things have been done and no time has been wasted with arguing then there is more time for playing and having fun together.

It is important:
<u>- to have a friendly attitude</u>
<u>- to stop using unfriendly words and sentences</u>
<u>- to let go of (endless) explanations and moral-preaching</u>

As I mentioned before language alone is not enough in itself but we can simply practise in the beginning.

I tried this practice out on my three teenagers at home. However, they realized what I was up to. My daughter immediately said: „Mum, stop this psycho-shit!" , and I started to laugh! – She had seen through it.   It was not easy but I stuck to it.

It was obvious that I was practising and not yet proficient.

**To be authentic you have to *mean* what you say.
Therefore it is good to find out what you really want.**

I could still improve and work on it. Also it is important to adapt the sentences to the age of the child. Also adults react positively to the constructive communication when we apply it correctly. The basics of the coco are applicable for children of all ages.
But sometimes we have to simply act, for example when there is danger.

**And sometimes it is more important or useful
to say nothing and just listen.**

A little anecdote: Medea, (4 years old) who had been in my play-group for some time, said one day (overhearing her mother and me talking about parenting and education):
„But Anahita, you don`t teach us at all!"
I laughed and said: „Ah, that`s very interesting!", and to the mother to set her at ease (so she would not think I didn`t 'teach' or 'educate' her child):
„Oh yes, certainly I do, but the children don`t realise it!"

Dumping Space
For the 'Present Day' Language

With 'present day' language I mean the conventional, often destructive language that we have been using up to now. **It is an advantage if we dump the present day language, because it either contains frightening words and sentences or is not corresponding to the truth.**

<u>Sentences and taboo-words for the trash-bin</u>

Taboo-words contain reproaches and express indirectly our own discontent.

never
must
should
ought to
always
finally
actually
at least
again
not even
a hundred times
good, bad, behaving, non-behaving
Here you can dump your own taboo-words:
-
-
-
-

Taboo-sentences are or contain:
reproaches, blaming, humiliation, everything that has to do with threatening, scolding, shouting at, preaching and belittling.

These words / sentences are creators of fear and when they reach the fear-centre in the brain they are consequently noxious and harmful.

Why don`t you listen?!
Not now! How often do I have to tell you??
Now it`s the last time that I have to tell you ...
Do I always have to tell you three, four times?!
How d`you say? What`s the magic word?! (Humiliating)
Can`t you ever do anything right?!/... finish anything?!"
Are you interested in anything at all?!
Do you have to make such a mess?!
Where are you with your thoughts again?!
Can`t you take a little more care?!
Where have you been?!
Why don`t you come home on time?!
How the heck could this happen?!
Didn`t I tell you, you should ...
Can`t you at least once ...
You still haven`t cleaned up this mess!
You always forget half of it!
Do you listen at all?!
And again you`re late!
You are completely nuts!
What`s happened?!
Look at yourself! It`s disgusting how you look!
Be careful so nothing goes wrong! (Increases the tension)
You never help me in the kitchen!
I have not deserved this! (Making yourself a victim)
Who do you think you are?!
I will never take you with me again!
You ruin the whole class!
Why are you talking such bullshit?!
I'll just give you one more chance! (Condescending)
It`s your own fault! Why weren't you more careful?!
That`s enough now! Stop crying immediately! (Harmful)
What are you up to?! (Are you asking out of fear?)

Now listen, this does not work! (This is not true, it has just worked out!)

Don`t ever do (say) this again! You hear me! Otherwise …! (Threatening)

Space for your own sentences to get rid of
-
-
-
-
-
-

From a taboo-list of harmful sentences, collected from parents themselves and as homework they were changed into **integrative** (golden)-sentences:

1. Why don`t you listen?!
> *„In our family we **listen to each other**."*

Using the 'we' form and including the child.

2. Not now!

   Telling exactly when gives the child a sensation of safety and trust.

   >*„At four o`clock we eat apples and bread. Can you wait together with me?"*

Communicating clearly, creating a connection.

3. How often do I have to tell you??
> *„**As soon as** you`ve cleaned up we can go to the beach together."*

Cheerful message.

4. This is the last time that I will tell you ...
> „What would you like to do first: brush your teeth or put on your pyjamas?"
Offering a choice between two.

5. Do I always have to tell you three, four times?
> **„What do you think?:** How long will it take you to finish playing? Three or five minutes?"
Requesting opinion and giving a choice.

6. How d`you say? What`s the magic word?
> „Grandma loves it when we thank her."

I always say thank you and so am a role model. **To force the child to say thank you will bring resistance rather than cooperation.** It will come by itself when we let it. The child knows the words, hears them from us and wants to imitate us, wants to belong.

Every greeting is a gift! When parents demand that their child greets me in order to reduce their own tension, so as not to shame the child , I tell them:

„We have already greeted each other with our eyes. This is sufficient for me."

We Always Take
Our Own Education With Us

The sentences we take with us from our own upbringing and which we normally use quite unconsciously, we have heard repeatedly. Although we think they are useful they usually contain threatening elements for children. They were commonly used as parents did not know any better. Formerly parents used threatening and punishment or the threat of punishment as a means for education. With this the fear-centre in the brain becomes activated which causes obedience out of fear and does not allow for free will. This (free will) was meant to be broken by the threatening – we can read about the 'poisonous pedagogy' (German Reich and before) as a recommendation in many old books!

Alternatively the child may rebel. There are tantrums; power-struggles arise, and aggressions occur. We label the children stubborn, obstinate or even 'pig-headed'. Parents and teachers can produce a long list of similar descriptions.

Fortunately, finally it was discovered that there is a reason behind all this behaviour: namely that the children would like to decide for themselves. We can call this phase of defiance the phase of autonomy. Actually it is not a phase but a time in which the reactions occur stronger. The word 'phase' is often used in a disparaging way: „It`s only a phase that will pass!" It is important to know that children rebel, give resistance or get aggressive because they defend themselves against our (too often occurring?) demands and orders against their will. How often do we demand something of them?

Indeed they have to defend themselves because of the urge to explore their surroundings, the world on their own, by themselves. To taste, feel and experience.

E*verything* is so powerful that they experience every 'no' as an injury against their integrity.

The reactions of the children are cries for help which we are obliged to hear.

Exceptions are - a constant whining which is a consequence of giving in too often and spoiling them.

With this response we make our children insecure: they don`t know what`s acceptable now.

First mum said 'no' and then she allows me all the same! The brain is learning: when I scream she gives in. Especially out and about, in the bus or supermarket! They will become more and more discontent and want more and more. In the end we cannot satisfy them any more at all. There arises a certain addictive behaviour. We shall come back to 'learn to endure' or 'bear it' for example in 'Good-bye' ... 50, Aggression ... 57 and 'Orders' ...76.

So we shouldn`t say 'no' anymore?
No, sure – because children need limits as they give them security. The boundaries should be as big and stable as possible. What I say is non-negotiable! No rubber-band-limits!
Yet with teenagers it means: to negotiate again and again anew. Widen your own borders as parents.
As small children are growing into the social network, into the community, they want to be part of the group and succeed in learning this. They learn faster and more happily, when we are firm and friendly.
The word 'actually' shows that there is always an exception. We can make humorous exceptions from time to time - if we really stand behind it and we honestly don`t mind. However, if it gets on our nerves and we only give in, in order to stop the whining of the child we have lost the battle and the child hasn`t gained anything except a little victory which it accepts together with our anger. What a pity for both!

What does 'integrative' mean?

**Integrative means
including all: 'as-well-as'
instead of being selective: 'either-or'.
Conventional parenting is judgmental,
integrative child-upbringing
is free from jdgement.**

Belonging, safety, tenderness, fondness:
Simone and Matteo

Constructive Communication – The 'Yes-Language'

If we could just hear what the little Indian girl is telling Khaleesi!

When I was studying to become an integrative teacher I chose a task: to practise saying „Yes, I know ..." for one week – every time I wanted to say 'no'. Here is the famous story that took place right at the beginning of my practice, which encouraged me so much that I stuck to it (I can say till now).
Instead of 'No' to say "Yes, I know ..." with loving understanding and consequent clarity.

Benni – from the Forest-Childcare

Benni was at my side: „Where are we going today?" „To the sun-place." „But I want to go to the shadow-place!" Now my practice started: a whole week of „Yes, I know" was before me. So I answered calmly: „Yes, I know you like the shadow-place." „Do we go to the shadow-place now?" „N- Yes I know you would very much like to go to the shadow-place. Today Helen (the assistant) and I have decided to go to the sun-place." I expected the usual tantrum and screaming and crying. Benni would so often throw himself on the ground and start screaming loudly, uttering shrill sounds and hitting out. Helen had taken the ladder-wagon already and gone ahead with all the other kids. As she was used to taking responsibility I had nodded towards her that I would take my time. The sun-place was not far away, and when she had arrived there she would let the children run around. They knew the place and had their favourite plays there. But Benni did not lie down on the ground; neither was he screaming around like he used to do before. No, he was just standing there, me beside him squatting at eye-level. He started to cry; first he was angry: "But I want to go to the shadow-place!" „Yes, my darling, I know! You would so much like to go there! You are so fond of this place! I am so sorry! Today we are going to the sun-place." His anger disappeared quickly; there remained only sorrow and disappointment. I let him cry, confirmed his sadness that we were going to a different place. After some time I could even take his hand. Very slowly again and again saying: „Yes, I know!" calmly and empathetically but at the same time staying firm that we went to the sun-place. I started moving hand in hand with Benni to the sun-place. Along the whole way he was crying but nevertheless coming with me. Over and over again we repeated our conversation and I was surprised how this developed. He was dissolving his whole resistance in his tears. His initial resentment (very short this time!) had quickly changed into redeeming grief and the tears cleaned disappointment, stress and frustration out of his body. I was deeply touched, also thankful and surprised at the effect of this exercise. When we arrived at the sun–place he let go of my hand and ran to the other kids.

With the „Yes, I know" he felt his feelings were acknowledged and accepted. He could accept that I stood by my first decision because he felt he had been taken seriously and because his feelings had been allowed. Important: I had neither distracted him nor given explanations nor given him promises. I had only stayed with his feelings. And I had not said: "Yes I know, but ..." (The "but" destroys everything positively that had been said before.)
An important part of integrative parenting is the 'Yes-language'. Here it is not simply about saying 'Yes' or „Yes, I know". Where would be the limits? I cannot always say yes to everything! Naturally not. It`s about

positive attention, the expression of positive-sentences. This means I have to think about what I want the child to do and express this. Most of us are used to expressing prohibitions: „Don`t do that! Don`t touch the jug! Don`t throw this vase down! Don`t climb this wall! Don`t tear so heavily!" The interesting part of this is that this message exists in two parts: one part reaches the right half of the brain and is transformed into a picture which is emotionally understood. (Jug, vase, wall and the action). The negotiation, the word 'not' does not transform into a picture, it reaches the left side of the brain and falls out immediately. There exists no connection between the picture and the abstract. So therefore the brain remembers the picture of the jug, the vase and the wall.

Sometimes we say: „Don`t go there! You will fall in!" Fatal when we realise that children not only want to fulfill our positive but also our negative expectations!

Some restrictions like „Let it be! Let go!" or „Don`t tear so fast!" or „Stop this!" are so abstract that the child does not know what it could do instead of this. It remains frustrated and helpless. It feels rejected, becomes sad or angry or starts to rage. The adults then say: „Oh well, now he/she is in the obstinate-phase!"

But there is no such phase. Being obstinate is a natural reaction to our restrictions where the child expresses his/her frustration and helplessness.

If we give clear directions, express what we want and give the child opportunities to act out what it wants, a lot of anger, rage and frustration can fall away on both sides and the child will automatically become more cooperative.

"We can caress the flower. Look here, the grass in the meadow you can pick!"

Substitute-option makes them happy!

"This jug wants to look down upon us from the shelf. You can use this plastic-bucket to draw water and water the plants."

Here we use the magic phase of the child. We make the jug a person. It wants to enjoy the wonderful view.

"The vase we put in the middle of the table together. From there all of us can look at it. Would you like a vase of your own for your flowers?"
"I want you to play down here in the grass. Could you do that?"
Just wait, don`t give an order.

"If you want to climb on the wall I would like to join. When I have finished raking the leaves I will come to you. I shall be even faster when you help me. You want to?"

Clearly I say what I want and suggest we work together. Children usually like to help and be involved.

"Ouch this hurts! You can comb or caress m͏· like this!"
I say what hurts and offer a sugge͏·
can choose instead; show the͏m ͏·

*"Ah, you really want to tear? ͏.
the shawl. You can tear this as m͏.*

Realise the real need of the child at this moment and offer a substitute so it can let out it`s frustrations without hurting itself or anyone else. Here a little anecdote from my playgroup:

Autumn-power
Laurin, (four years old) who has an older brother and a newborn sibling as well, hits a carton-box that lies on the ground with a wooden cudgel. I confirm:
„Yes, here you can hit very hard, show your strength and letting it out." He is beaming and carries on hitting. Then he stops and tells me:" I am even getting stronger from doing this, it keeps coming!"

He is right. What leaves the body, can be anger or frustration which, when suppressed in the body holds back energy.

When we let go of our emotions, blockades open up and the genuine constructive power is set free.

How many times a day do you think a toddler might hear the word 'no'? Even if we don`t know the true answer we can guess that the number is very high!
A baby usually gets the attention that it needs in its first year and is thought to be by most people, lovely and cute. It is admired, pampered and looked at in wonder. Rarely enough is it denied a wish and this is correct so: it is not possible to spoil a child until the eighth month. It has its needs which have to be met. It is helplessly exposed to us grown-ups. Besides its hunger to be satiated and its thirst to be quenched, changing nappies and cleaning the body it is in need of tenderness, care and touch. They need to be held, hugged, kissed, caressed, talked to, sung to, carried

around, body-contact and many friendly contacts. In parent-training the participants always work out a long list of contributions. Normally we know the needs of a baby and are able to fulfil them.

When the child is a year old and starts moving around everything changes in an instant. What changes most is your face! The drama starts when it stands up on its legs and starts the first uneasy steps, exploring the world which first only consists of a few rooms.

If the home is not prepared for the child and adapted to the child's safety and our needs, a catastrophe is about to enter into our lives. We know how this works: „No, not the computer! No, leave that flower-pot! No, the vase! No no! Daddy`s book! Oh no, grannies knitting! Oh no, not my glasses again! No, no, kaka! Don`t touch the potty! It`s yucky!"

There is this story of a little girl named Suzie that heard her parents say all day long: "Suzie, let be!" When she was asked what was her name she answered:
„Suzie Letbe!"

Until the child comes to a play-group and later to a kindergarten it has heard so many 'no' words that it has stored up a lot of anger inside. Every 'no' is a brake; it means slowing the child or stopping its natural urge to explore.

It has to touch, grab, grasp, hold onto, turn around, knock, put everything in its mouth, taste, smell, smear, try out, with all its senses it wants to 'touch' the world and its surroundings. „To get in touch with" means really to be touched by something, means to understand with the whole body. Only then can the brain build deep synapses and the experiences can be understood and saved in the brain mostly forever.

Therefore every 'no' brings up anger, frustration and despair, so you cannot expect cooperation from the child. If we force the child to do what we want it to do it can either show more resistance, or their self-will becomes broken and the child discouragingly surrenders. It would be an advantage for the parent if the child cooperates from its own free will and from understanding.

This is not possible for the toddler because the brain develops this cognitive capacity only at about the third year of life. Therefore as soon as they start crawling around we take everything that they should not touch, out of their reach and enrich the immediate surroundings of the toddlers on the floor with interesting and safe things which they can explore without limits and with pleasure. In my kitchen I always had an extra drawer with harmless kitchen-utensils ready with which the children could play at my feet. From time to time I added one more thing to keep it exciting, and later I let them help me more and more with my tasks in the household and kitchen.

Sergej`s joy: the discovery of noise-music

The Acknowledgement of Brain-Research

The integrative method benefits from brain-research. A human being`s emotions are only reached through the 'right side' of the brain - the Amygdala, the almond-kernel. Creativity, language, colour, intuition, and philosophy are processed here too. In simple terms we can divide it into the joy-centre and the fear- or self-rewarding-centre. The fear-centre is reached when in the conventional way one is scolded, shamed, blamed, threatened, exposed or in any other way punished.

When the fear-centre is reached in the child, he/she has three main-possibilities for reaction:

- Running away: flight. This can happen inwardly (retreating) or outwardly. The child does not want to learn.
- Feigning death: becoming passive, becoming 'dull', not saying anything anymore, feigning indifference, wanting to be left alone (the fourth step of the 'four erroneous goals' ... 39).
- Attacking: stepping into the power-struggle, aggression against parents and teachers (second and third step of the 'four mistaken goals').

Sometimes children choose illness to escape all of this. Then they can stay in bed and are cared for (hopefully). This happens unconsciously. In any case, it is destructive and useless for the relationship with the child when this fear-centre is activated. So before saying something or acting, always ask yourself: which centre will be stimulated through my action?

In all the best situations, the neurotransmitter Dopamine is released from the 'self rewarding centre'. This happens when we experience success, when we feel part of, integrated in and accepted by the community. When we are approved of we experience joy. When we feel taken seriously, respected, and paid attention to we feel recognized. Our true nature having been seen, supported and encouraged. So our basic needs are fulfilled.

These are inter alia: attention, care, tenderness, freedom of movement, self-determination, esteem and freedom of expression. Being allowed to have an opinion, to co-determine, to choose, to have friends, to express creativity and to allow imagination. To have the space for development and the possibility to do things at one's own speed and in one's own time. So, if we want children to listen to us, to behave cooperatively and to follow our directions we need to talk to the 'right side' of their brain. To dial 'the correct number' so that we can make a connection.

Hence this connection to the child is very important because the child is learning through the relationship. *Education is relation.* Most children learn for the sake of the grown-ups. When the child feels accepted and loved it wants to learn. The production of Dopamine brings about the wish to get 'more of that'. Where the child has been successful it will try again with enthusiasm. Motivation originates from inside. It always arises from inside, never externally. However, it is fostered through outer circumstances. If the child is pleased with how it is handled and likes our intonation it will love to be there to play and learn. The left side of the brain, which is in charge of logical thinking is activated later on at about seven years of age. So if we ask cognitive questions, for example, using w-words such as 'why, when, who, what, which or how?' they will lead you away from the child's feelings and you will not be able to reach the child emotionally. Therefore they are better avoided in situations of conflict. How did this happen? What has happened? Who has started this? Who is responsible for that? Whose fault is this? Who is to blame? Why do you always do that? Why did you do that? Why can`t you ...! Mostly they are accusations at the same time which can activate the fear-centre again. When something has happened we enquire of the child's feelings and give them space. (Refer to 'The Integrative Dealing With Feelings' pages 33 and 103).

We concentrate on what is going well and emphasize that. Make more of the positives so that joy emerges as well as the desire to accomplish more. This is because it is so pleasurable (not because the child has to).

We can obtain optimal success when we activate both halves of the brain and intertwine them so that they are linked together.

The addition of music, singing and movement in nature offers more possibilities for positive connections. Be it with both hands and feet, the whole body through dancing, with the voice or with an instrument. It lies in our hands to make child 'education' a wonderful experience with all of the senses so that the synapses 'explode' from growing and spreading joy and enthusiasm!

But... it requires our own motivation.

Gerald Hüther, a German brain-scientist talks of the 'watering-can-principle' – in my opinion a striking metaphor!

**When we ourselves are enthusiastic
this energy is passed on to the children.**

Yasha and Aaliyah give a good example here!

We can also see the copying of the mime below.

The Integrative Dealing with Feelings

1. Allowing (all feelings)
2. Naming (using questions)
3. Letting it happen (expressing)
4. Redirecting if necessary
   (using the energy constructively)

1. Allowing all feelings:
This process takes place inside oneself: it is an accepting attitude towards all that exists.
All feelings are allowed, and are okay merely because they exist. Feelings never ever arise without reasons even if we cannot see them. Sometimes these reasons lie far back in the past. Something what happens now is only a trigger but maybe never the original cause.
I also allow my own feelings to arise; I feel them and practise coping with them. I also name them.
'Yes'-sentences have a healing effect.

Sadness, grief:
„Yes, cry, it will do you good!"
„Yes, this makes you sad!"
Anger, rage, frustration:
„Yes, let it out! Show me how angry you are!"
„Yes really, this is an awkward unbearable frustration!"
„Yes this is bothering you! "

Fear:
Fear is a natural and very important feeling and absolutely normal. Fear warns us of danger and tells us that something is wrong. The sentence: „There is no need to be frightened" is absolutely senseless and destructive. (The child is already afraid!)

The child feels „I am in the wrong". Saying that even I am sometimes frightened can relieve the child. Or, that I had also been frightened in a similar situation. Then the encouragement starts:
„We can learn a lot from what we are afraid of."
and
"What we fear we practise even more."

I then guide the child mindfully to the challenge:
„Where do you want to start? What do you want to start with?"
Maybe the child can choose and make the first step itself.

<u>Joy:</u>
„How lovely to see you are so happy! It makes me happy too!"
Be aware of thoughts like "This won`t last long, anyway!" and see how as a child you learned to dim joy in order not to get hurt. Allow also joy to flow freely!

2. Naming the feelings:
This I do by asking questions in order not to force something or impose an idea on the child (or person). First I check that I have interpreted correctly. If it is perfectly clear it is also okay to just name it.

Example: the child is crying.
„Are you sad?"
It stamps with its feet and shouts angrily: „No!"
„So, you are angry! Yes, sometimes I am also really mad!"

Important: no 'w'-questions (why? what? when? where? who?) These appeal the left side of the brain, so no emotional connection can develop.

We dial the 'correct telephone-number' by reacting to the feelings of the child, not to the circumstances. That comes in later. First the child wants to be emotionally 'endorsed' 'under*felt*' instead of 'understood' (an expression by Mària Kenessey), *then afterwards* understood. When the feelings are felt through till the end, till they are really over, accepted and expressed, a circle closes. Relaxation, silence, peace and a deep satisfaction arise. Then the child can tell you how it all happened (if it is still needed).

Maybe you know this process. When you have gone through a really deep crisis with all your feelings being outwardly expressed or inwardly intensely felt over a longer time, and then, when you have not held anything back, it suddenly subsides and becomes still. Then deep peace and bliss can occur.

3. Allowing the feelings to be expressed:

After naming them verbally I give the feelings now a wider physical space in and outside the body.

<u>Sadness, Grief:</u>

Tears are washing stress-hormones out of the body; so the permission is part of the healing-process. If tears and sadness are stopped, physical illnesses can result or an increase in the symptoms can occur. Something will be 'fermenting' deeper inside the child.

In the following song-text painful experiences such as children know and have, are sung. I allow crying and reassure the child: "If you want I can comfort you".

There are children who cannot bear being touched throughout the mourning-process. I always wait until he/she wants to be comforted. But to comfort does not mean to quickly discard the sadness!

Cry, it will do you good

> **1.** Have you ever banged your head?
> Given nasty blames?
> Did your play-mates pester you?
> Did they call you names?
> **Ref. Cry, oh cry, it will do you good**
> Let the tears appear,
> If you want I'll caress you,
> Let the tears now flow.
> Cry, oh cry, it will do you good
> Let the tears appear,
> If you want I'll caress you,
> Later you will be glad.

Later you will be glad:
This gives the child time. The child does not have to recover and be glad quickly as a reward to us grown-ups who tend to have difficulties dealing with children's sadness. It is our own grief that is awakened which probably had to be suppressed when we were children.

Anger:
It takes a bit of courage and imagination to let out anger constructively. I discuss with the children where in the body the anger might be located and wants to come out.
Second stanza of the song:

2. Did they laugh and shout at you,
Because you are different from them?
Did they take your toys and break them
Did they throw them away in the trash?

Ref.: Ref. Cry, oh cry, it will do you good
Let the tears appear,
If you are angry it`s okay,
Let the anger come out!
Cry, oh cry, it will do you good
Let the tears appear,
If you are angry it`s okay,
Later you will be glad.

Some locations of anger in the body:
In the arms
shows by hitting, pushing, boxing etc. Work out by hitting at the surrounding air, pushing out or rowing, doing hard work, boxing into a bag or cushion.
In the hands
shows by hitting, scratching, pinching etc.
In the throat
comes out when we shout, scream, whimper, roar, swear.
In the legs and feet
when they kick, trample, dance, hop, jump.

At home the sofa will do or a mattress that you can hit. There are soft balls you can offer on these occasions that can be thrown around, called *stress-balls.*
You could also provide an *anger-cushion.*
(I have bought them in charity shops.)
You could even use a genuine boxing- bag!

4. Redirect the feelings when required:
When it looks like getting dangerous I offer, as mentioned above, a substitute to let out the anger or direct the power into an action that needs strength.

Important! Redirecting is not diverting.

The feeling(s) arising should be allowed to stay present. We stay alert and make sure nobody comes to any harm. When younger children hit out at each other I just show them what I want instead of the hitting: aha, aha, caress, caress. I caress both of their heads if they allow me to - they usually do. If a child loves to bite I offer them a ball or ring of hard rubber.

In the play-group I act out together with the children - hitting the mats, trampling, stamping and shouting:

„I am so angry, angry, yes, I am so angry!"

The mother of a boy in my playgroup told me she now does this 'on the go' or when they are out shopping. When she gets angry because of her boys' behaviour and she is likely to lose her temper, she stops and stamps. Afterwards she feels much better. Courageous! This is a good role-model for the kids too. Or you could just imagine yourself doing it: be intensively aware of your emotions and take them seriously - without reacting. Just breathe deeply and stay with it.

**It is important that every person finds his or her own strategy and that you do what suits you.
Then you are authentic and will succeed.**

Using the power constructively:
"You have a lot of power in your arms! I wonder whether you can help me pull that wagon!"

„Just now I need help to tidy up the chairs. What do you think? Would you have enough strength to do that? Do you think you`ll manage?"

The Four Erroneous Goals of the Child According to Mària Kenessey And Rudolf Dreikurs

With constant discouragement and a feeling of exclusion the child can develop disorders which are magnified by the extent of its despair. And truly it only wants to be loved and is seeking its place in the group.

> First goal: Wanting to get attention.
The unconscious belief of the child: „I am loved only when I get (constant) attention."
It accepts humiliation or punishment, puts up with being sent away rather than being ignored because being ignored is more hurtful then being blamed, punished or even spanked.
Emotion of the adult: The child is a 'nuisance', 'bothersome'. We feel bothered, irritated, annoyed, and impatient.

The way forward (stepping out of the old):
be aware of your 'instant' reactions and let them go: „Stop it! Stop bothering me! Can`t you leave me alone for at least five minutes! If you don`t, then …!"
Get rid of this old rubbish!
Give encouragement instead, which means: give your one hundred percent attention to the child for a certain time (if necessary agree beforehand for how long).
Show your approval, be friendly and kind when the child is not 'misbehaving'. (Giving positive attention.)

After having given attention you set a limit:

„I am now going to make a ten minute call to grandma. What would you like to do while I am on the phone? I wonder if you will be able to do that for ten minutes? Here is the clock. If you want you can say hello to her first."

You can also expect this from younger children. Show them the time with the hands of the clock.

Give them praise in form of appreciation:

„Great! This time you were successful for three minutes. Let`s see how many you can do next time!"

Show them trust-in-advance:

„I am sure that this will get better and better!"

Don`t make it into a competition with others ("Your bigger brother could do this much better at your age!") No comparison (this would be humiliating, shaming and discouraging).
It is very helpful to give important jobs, responsibilities, duties and errands. It is not helpful to give put downs because the child will feel humiliation. The child wants to contribute equally and play its part.

If possible do not describe or talk about or act to the undesired behaviour.

> Second goal: Wanting to be right in the end (power and control)

The unconscious opinion of the child: only if I win am I 'good enough'. (Contradiction, wanting to win, constantly having power-struggles).

Adults react slightly irritated or angry to this. They think or feel: "*I* want to win!" "*I* want to be right in the end!"

The way forward (stepping out of the old):
abandon certain sentences and destructive words as well as demands and prohibitions: "I told you no! Let the piano be! Don`t hit the Xylophone so hard! You break everything! No, you won`t get an ice-cream now!"

Children that always want to contradict or undermine have already heard too many 'no' responses and have been given many orders or refusals. They want to be understood and included.

„What is your opinion? Will it rain today? What do you prefer? What shall we do first? Go into the park or do the shopping? Cooking spaghetti or making baked potatoes?"

Remember to keep your sense of humour. Judo instead of boxing means using the child`s energy.

> Third goal: Wanting to take revenge
The unconscious opinion of the child: they don`t love me! It hurts! I also want to hurt! I want you to feel my pain, my suffering, my despair!

These behaviours are pushing, scratching, hitting, biting (with younger children).

With older ones: ganging up, being ´mean´, lying, stealing, ruining things ...

Reaction of the adult: wanting to shake the child. The so-called harmless smack on the bottom or on the fingers can evoke different reactions but in any case it is harmful. What if we think about our role as a model for the children? The brain is learning: I see the big ones can hit the small ones. Besides that, the child feels completely misunderstood because it acted out of its distress: it feels unloved and does not know how to show this any other way. After this kind of response the child's behaviour is bound to get worse.

The way forward (stepping out of the old):

dispense with w-words, threatening and blaming sometimes disguised in questions: „ Who started this?!" „Why did you do this?! What have you done again?! Where did you get this stick? Why do you have to punch others?!" „You wait till daddy gets home!" „If you bite one more time!"
So instead: comfort the crying child or hold them both in a caring way. Comfort and soothe them. Talk to them - always adapting the language to their age:

„Ouch, yes, this hurts!"
Recognise the feelings of both - not separating them into victim and aggressor. Both are feeling hurt!

„Are you sad? Are you angry?
Do you have a problem with each other / Have you had an argument?"
Use language that connects with them so they feel that you understand.
In the play-group:
Trust the children to have conflict-solving-competence:

„So...what do you think? Can you have a successful argument by yourselves or do you need some help?"

"Can you discuss it to a good end? I am sure, you will find a solution."

Asking the other children:
„What do you think Andy needs? What does he need to feel more comfortable in this group? Have you got an idea?"
Then the child will feel understood. It is not exposed; it gets sympathy from its friends and from the grown-ups.
Mirroring the child's feelings, showing empathy, letting the child experience success, integrating the child like this into the group can bring about miracles.

> Fourth goal:
Withdrawal, helplessness and inadequacy
The unconscious opinion of the child: I am unworthy, inadequate and incapable. Don`t ask anything of me and please don`t ask any questions, I don`t know the answers anyway!
Sensation of the grown-ups: helplessness, feeling pity.

<u>The way forward (stepping out of the old)</u>:
ask no questions that 'highlight' their own helplessness. In other words notice consciously and accept what you see. Maybe even describe how you feel:
„I have no idea how I could possibly help you!
I really feel helpless!
If I only knew what you needed ..."

Reassuring:
„Here with me, nobody is forced to do or say anything. We have so much time."

Recognise achievements and focus on past successes.
"Now this is getting better every time."
No pity - but empathy!
Pity means feeling *sorry for* the child: „Oh dear, you poor thing!" This harms the child because it takes away its strength and competence. The child should be able to regain its self-confidence and get the idea that it is able to decide for itself.
Empathy means feeling *with* the child:
"Yes, this feels awful. Yes, sometimes even I don`t know what to do!"

Summary:
Depending on our practice and attitude as well as the language we choose to use, the negative behaviours can be reinforced or cured. If we show the child the (unconsciously) desired response at the onset it will be shortly satisfied it has 'won'. Unfortunately through punishment, exclusion and reprimand the child feels even more discouraged and unloved. Then he/she has to repeat his/her misguided behaviours which makes everything worse. However, no child is able to step out of this vicious circle alone, they surely need our help!
So if we can react differently and not as expected we frustrate the child's efforts in a positive way:
The expected negative attention does not arrive. After the child's vain attempt it can give up this course of action. The child is not in need of it any more. It feels it belongs, it feels loved and integrated!

**This is an essential part of integrative education.
I would even refer to it as the foundation
upon which everything else is built!**

What children need: body-contact, tenderness, safety, care

Summary – What We Can Do; How We Can Optimise Our Relationships

We can optimize our relationships by:
Acting instead of talking
Addressing feelings
Facilitating success instead of describing catastrophes
Asking oneself: What happened before? What did the child achieve with its action? What can I change?
Asking opinions
Bearing it
Being a role-model
Being affectionate
Being on eye-level
Being patient
Coming to a positive conclusion
Considering mistakes as friends (no correcting)
Counting to 30 (before reacting)!
Empathising
Exploring (the behaviour of our children and ourselves)

Friendliness, friendly language
Friendly natural consequences instead of punishing and threatening
Giving appreciation
Giving attention
Giving ultimate freedom within clear limits
Giving time
Giving trust-in-advance
Holding the magnifying glass over the goals that have been reached
Humour, parenting with humour, laughing about oneslf
Incorporating the child into our activities and duties
Integrating instead of being selective
Keeping promises
Letting them help
Loving! (Starting with yourself)
Not noticing undesirable behaviour
Observing
Offering a substitute (after every STOP an OPTion)
Parenting more carefully (more awareness)
Pointing out the positive side
Reaching the joy-centre (self-rewarding-centre)
Setting limits
Supporting
Saying „Yes, I know …" instead of constantly 'No' (Keeping 'No' or 'Stop!' for emergencies)
Taking breaks
Taking a break from parenting (you and the children deserve it!)
Tenderness
Thinking and acting in an integrative way instead of selectively
Thinking and acting imaginatively instead of being focused on the negative

Using constructive communication
Using the 'Yes-language' (defining what you want)
Using 'We-sentences'
Waiting

Music!
Allowing and sharing joy in an Indian train

List of Miracle Words

Miracle words are those that enable us to feel good, comfort us, and make us happy. They reach the joy-centre of the brain and allow the happiness hormone Dopamine to be produced. This then brings about the joy that strengthens our connections with each other, enriching the relationship, and facilitates a feeling of belonging and safety.

Great!
Fantastic!
Wonderful!
Amazing!
Knocks me out!
Excellent!
I am enthusiastic about this! I just love it!
I am so proud of you!
Great that you are here!
I am so sorry!
Luckily!
Doesn`t matter!
This can happen!
Terrific!
Awesome!
Incredible!
Yes!

Add on more,
as many as you can
find and like!

You can make yourself a much more colourful and bigger list and hang it onto the fridge.

Our magic miracle words
....
....
....
....
....
....
....
....
....
....
....
....
....
....
....
....
....
...

We use the miracle words and golden sentences to reach the child where it can decide for itself that it wants to cooperate!

Contact by the eyes, waving and a smile

Kareem, Pratibha and Khaleesi in Goa, India

Concrete Examples in the Use of 'Golden Sentences'

Themes

Good-bye, Farewell, Cutting the Umbilical Cord

From my play-group-letter:

Saying goodbye and moving on is a gradual process over time:
Repeatedly we part and find each other again. The child is learning: **I am allowed to be sad and cry and I can bear it**. The child is growing in this knowledge, becoming stronger and more courageous. This process strengthens its feeling of self-esteem, courage and its ability to trust. It is healthy for children to discover that there are other nice friendly people who will care for them, play with them, feed and love them.
New associations and relationships are growing. They are a good base for the future.

Saying goodbye to parents will be easier for the child if it repeatedly hears (joyfully) in advance that it *can* visit the play-group because it is now *old enough.*
How lovely it will be there where it can play with other children, do handicrafts, paint, draw and sing. The teacher is looking forward to welcoming the child.
This is what it is: a present for your child.
At the same time it is important to feel your own sadness and ask yourself: am I ready to let go of my child already? When I am prepared for it inwardly my child will be able to do it as well.

„Are you very sad? Yes, cry, let it out."
„Let the tears flow, it does you so much good!"
„Yes I know, I love you very much too!"
„Come here and hold me tight one more time!"
„I am leaving now and will be back at half past eleven.
I am already looking forward to seeing you soon!"
„Yes, I love you very much too!"
„Yes, I will also miss you a lot!"
And then: really leave!

Preparing by 'looking forward' to go to the grandparents:

„Grandma and grandpa are looking forward to seeing you again! What did you play with them last time? The bear in your bed there is waiting and longing to see you!"

It is better not to give a lot of annoying advice to **older children** when they part for a journey.
It is much more useful to give them trust-in-advance and wish them well:

„Have a lovely time! – I am so proud of you!"
„Have a good journey – enjoy!"
„Have fun!"

Rather than: „Be careful!", this causes stress. Taking care is included in your wish that they enjoy themselves. It is our own fears that are present. We should simply feel them, be with them and keep them in this moment. Maybe later there will be the opportunity to tell the kids about our feelings.

Aggression:
Biting, Scratching, Hitting, Pushing and Screaming

First of all it is good that anger is allowed to come out. When aggressive emotions stay in the body they can do a great deal of harm there in time.

Secondly, aggression derives from the Latin verb 'aggredior' and means to approach, address! (Attack).

Thirdly, when children bite, scratch, hit, push or scream they are showing us their helplessness.

Spanking shows that grownups have run out of ideas and don't know what else to do.

However, the difference is that adults can stop and control themselves but children are still at the learning stage. We, as adults are role-models and show children how we deal with our own anger. Do we let it out on others? Or can we find a better way so that nobody gets hurt? This is what I mean when I say 'having it under control' that we can **redirect the anger but not suppress it!** (Imagine a volcano being suppressed!)

It helps to be aware of, to perceive, to name and express feelings:

„Oh dear, right now I am really angry! I 'll go jogging!"
„I am so frustrated, I'll take a walk."
or: *„I'll retreat to the bathroom for a while."*
„When I come back, we will find a solution together!"
Giving them 'trust-in-advance'.

„Now this is too much for me. Please go to your rooms and come back when you have finished quarrelling and it's really over!"
Let them go through their whole process.

Younger children often bite. Sometimes there is despair behind this behaviour: the child is not yet able to express itself or has not yet mastered language. The child is therefore frustrated because it would like to talk to others but is not understood. So the child communicates in a very intensive way, for example through biting.

Biting in itself is very pleasurable, joyful!

Well yes, also painful. The toddler does not know this, yet. We can let it bite into its own arm so it can feel how it feels. Mostly once is sufficient then it will understand and stop biting. It is important to offer a substitute though. With older children we can ask them and search with them for something in the toy-box that they could bite into, in an emergency. One mother put a necklace with a biting-ring around her daughter`s neck so that she could have the ring with her all the time. This girl was about two years old and was biting children when they came too close, when she felt stressed (fear), when she wanted to keep something (threat), or when her mother was talking to another child (jealousy).

I suggested this mother stayed very close to her daughter for the next three weeks, especially at the beginning of playtime on the playground or when the family had visitors so as to touch and caress her repeatedly and often. When the child ventured away by herself it would be good to just keep an eye on her and say nothing so as not to interrupt her play. When other children approached she should move nearer unobtrusively and stretch her hand in between the two children as soon as the next bite looks like coming.

If the bite has already happened to not blame her as this increases the tension.

The child should be able to relax, feeling safer and safer so that it can let go of this habit.
It is important to comfort the child who has been bitten. Caress and comfort both children – what do we have two hands for? Do not overdo the attention but it can be helpful to draw a (friendly!) consequence:

„What a pity. Now we shall go home. Tomorrow you can try again. When you are angry you can bite into your ring. You know this. We will practise this more! I am confident that you will be successful!"

Providing safety and comfort *at the beginning* of this learning and in-between is advantageous.
Strengthening the self-esteem repeatedly as we give them work to do, letting them help us:

„I am so proud of you!"
„You are my big girl!"
„It is fantastic how you just know when to give me a hand! (to help me)."

*„Ouch this hurts! You can **bite the rubber-ball**."*
*„Stop, this hurts! You can **hit the anger-cushion**,"*
(the couch etc. – having talked about this before-hand, 'Emotional Education') boxing-bag or mats.

With humour and „magic":

*„Are you a wild cat? Would you like to scratch the carpet and sharpen your tiger-claws there?
Would you like to play lion with me?"*
*„Show me your claws!
Wow! Should I be afraid?"*

*"We can take the **scream**-test.*
We'll count to three together, then you can scream very loud; for whom it is too loud can close their ears during this 'screaming-time'.
Then I will catch the sounds in my hands – like this. (You can also agree upon a different sign to stop).
Okay, let`s go: one – two – three!"
Limit: "Now this is too loud for me. Now you can scream in your own room till you are done (finished)."
"In our family we are friendly to each other. Would you like to help me (you could help me / I could do with some help) to push the chairs / to stack them up ...)"
"Could you help me carry the box of mineral water bottles out of the cellar? Do you think you can do that? Are you strong enough for that?"
"I don`t want you to hurt yourself or others. Where (How) could you let out your anger?"

Doing something useful with the energy and letting them have experiences of success, boosts their (now low) self-esteem. Integrate them - let them be part of what is happening, make them feel important and give them responsibility.

What to do when children **scream in public** because they don`t get what they want:
If your nerves are strong enough:

"Yes, let it out. I am here."
Stay close, maybe touching the child gently, if it allows. Remember to be aware of the child's physical space and possible response to defend itself.
Be friendly - assuring people who make remarks, want to give you advice or help you:

„Everything is okay, we are in control of what`s happening here!"
or
„Thank you for your helpful advice!"
or
„How nice that your children don`t ever do this!"
Stay calm!
When it is becoming too much for you, take the child and leave:

„This is enough for today, we are going home. When you think you know how to behave we can try again tomorrow."

Sometimes it can help to reflect on what happened before the event - the antecedent. Did I promise something and not keep it?
If it is about rules that the child does not want to obey and tries to get what it wants through a tantrum stay calm:

"Yes I know you want another lolly-pop right now. I am sorry, you've already had one today. Tomorrow you can have another one ."

'You can' is better than 'you may' because the latter is suggesting a condition and power over the other. With this there would not be equality.
Let go of long explanations - they only lead to endless discussions or the child does not listen anymore anyway. The child's perception: How stupid do they think I am? I know this already!
When we have clear instead of elastic boundaries we give the child security and something to adhere to.

It knows a promise will be kept. The child is allowed to show and express its frustration about it though.
We can relax when we know that. When we realise that we don`t have to persuade or convince children. Mostly this would only create ill-humour and end up with hateful compromises and discontent on both sides. Who does not know these feelings? – 'They are simply doing what they want! They always get what they want!'
We can practise **clarity and firmness**. We can ask ourselves: What do I really want? What is really important to me? Discuss, find a common level with him / her.
What helps usually - going outdoors often and regularly and letting them play in nature!

> **And then - just putting up with it, bearing it!**
> **It is not easy but rewarding!**
> **Actually it is just simple!**

Part of a song:
'Row, row, row your boat gently down the stream.
If you see a crocodile, don`t forget to: screeeaaam!'
Play fierce!
It is great and makes you feel so strong!

Fear

Fear is an important function to warn us: it shows when there is something wrong and alerts us to dangers. Therefore the sentence: „There is no need to be afraid!" is annoying, senseless and discouraging. The child is already frightened, facing the fear and trying to cope with it. Give the child an 'you are okay feeling', let it feel it is of equal value:

„Yes, sometimes I am also afraid."
„When I was your age I was afraid of ..."

Connecting with the child:
„Little by little we practise what frightens us until we are successful."

Encourage, give 'trust-in-advance':
„You will see it will get easier and easier.
Daring to make small steps strengthens the ability to make decisions:
„What do you want to begin with? There is no need to attempt everything today." (Setting at ease)

Taking the feeling seriously:
„A ghost underneath your bed? What does it look like? What does it want? Do you want to let the door open a little bit? We will leave a light on in the corridor during the night. I shall also leave my door open so I can hear you."

Using the imagination, creating a caring connection:
„A crocodile? Come on, let`s feed it. Then it will be full and can sleep, too."

Getting dressed (Autonomy)

Mira has (fine) motor difficulties and does not like to dress by herself. She gives up quickly, saying that she cannot do it. Her mother Bernadette is getting impatient and grumbles that Mira is old enough and should be able to do it on her own by now: „When you go to kindergarten you will have to ... (It is the mother`s fear that is actually preventing the child).
Mira needs to feel relaxed and to be trusted to do it.
So does her mother, first of all for herself.
Calm down: there is still time!
Giving trust-in-advance:
„We will do it before you start kindergarten.
Which piece would you like to put on all by yourself today?"
„Maybe you`d like me to sing the jumping Jack-song, see what he`s putting on? Ok, jumping Jill ..."

Allow the child to do so without too many suggestions. Give time - and more time. Use the clock; show the long and the short hand - the passage of time. Make a schedule, use drawings.
Here is some feedback from parents who have introduced the clock with a plan: „Since we get up fifteen minutes earlier everything is working much better. We don`t have so much stress any more. The children have an alarm-clock and have responsibility."
"Since I have introduced the clock everything works out fine. I have drawn a schedule with the children and hung it up. They always go and look at it to see how far they have got already. They want to be faster every morning, helping each other, wanting to beat the clock!"

Yes, there is obviously less stress and more pleasure.
Another 'getting-dressed' problem solved by the child:
Vera's mother Tanja scolds her: „You always want to put on what you want! It is so annoying!" So Vera says: „Here is the anger-cushion!" and brings it to her mother. (At that time Vera was about two years old!) Tanja (already following the 'integrative parenting training') reacted spontaneously by hitting the cushion and shouting: "I am angry!" and Vera grins.

Katja puts stickers on the drawers - drawings of what is inside them. Joelle (her daughter) takes out what she needs the evening before. In the morning Katja is helping Joelle get dressed. What an excellent idea! (Katja is beaming, at least she had 'done something right once'! Her self-criticism and self-doubt are very high.) I mentioned Maria Montessori: if Katja wrote the word beside the picture her daughter could read and learn the letters at the same time. Or – even better – she could let her daughter write them herself.

In the mornings Betty helps her daughter Anne get dressed, calmly and in a matter of fact way which simply means Betty dresses Anne whilst she is still lying in her bed. On the weekends it is not an issue at all, there is no hurry and Anne puts on her clothes all by herself.

An example in the playgroup:

Should we help the children get dressed?
We have eaten our snacks and start to get dressed to go out. With winter-jackets and trousers this is quite an issue! Fleece-jackets, jumpers, mittens, boots and hats. Very soon the three girls are ready to go. The boys are standing around

helplessly, messing around, creating diversions; they have no idea whether it is the front or back of their trouser legs or if sleeves are inside out. Helping? No, the girls won`t help.

If I intervene now I will slip into the mother-role, and this could be a problem. But I have to, if we still want to go outdoors!

I was searching to find different solutions: the girls could help the boys; when finished the girls could get dressed as well. My partner confirmed that this was also the procedure at the military training establishment.

So, the next time I announced that we would try it like that. The girls agreed. The boys were then informed of how the procedure would work. I busied myself with other things and didn't interfere. It worked fantastically. The girls each chose a boy. One of the boys avoided being helped and got dressed very quickly on his own. Now the other boy had two female helpers!

The next time I noticed a change.

One of the boys dressed all by himself as before and got ready immediately. The other boy accepted help from both girls but tried to start on his own. Obviously so much physical closeness and attention was getting too much for him. The third one, the youngest, cried and wanted to get to me. I pretended to be very busy and repeatedly pointed to his helper. This one really did her job very well. I made sure that she was not teasing him, no, he was crying, because he`d prefer me. He was relatively new in the group and I found it a good opportunity for him to have contact with others. In the meantime I encouraged him:

„You are doing very well, Michael, you see, Sonja is an excellent helper! Lovely, how you two are managing this together!"

Finally they were all dressed and we went out into the snow.

This event had an additional positive side-effect: Sonja (of Italian origin) used to be dressed by her mother, not moving a finger herself. Now, in this situation Sonia gradually takes

responsibility, dresses herself and then, just like her mother knows exactly how to dress another child!
She has experienced this herself so many times that she can do it to somebody else perfectly! And Michael has quickly become used to her; she has always been very friendly to him!

(Translated from the book „Die integrative Erziehung im Vorschulalter" by Anahita Huber)

Most beautiful integrative possibility getting up and getting dressed:

"Good morning, my darling! Do you already know what you want to wear today?"
"Oh mummy, yes. Most of all I want to wear YOU!"

Lending an open ear to a child is so rewarding for both!

Tasks, Jobs, Responsibilities, Family-Council

How much we would like everybody to assist in the household! As a mother of three teenagers I thought that this would happen voluntarily! In time I learned how I could succeed in getting them to make up their own minds and choose their responsibilities. We can achieve this quite well with a family get together or family activity once a week at a fixed time.

Family council – a secret success-recipe

Round 1 : **Circle of appreciation**
This round was called 'compliment-round' in a home for teenagers and it has changed the climate and the behaviour enormously. In the beginning it was a bit awkward for the youngsters but they adapted quickly to saying something positive about each other.
In Manager-training this 'showering' is also used: at the end of a seminar all participants are showered individually with positive feedbacks.
A pure 'endorphin charged' phenomenon!
Adults are the models of this technique and think beforehand what family members have done that has contributed to a pleasant family-life.
The appreciations should be expressed mainly positively and as 'I-messages' (without using 'not'). If this happens we correct by repeating the sentence positively. Gradually the children will do it automatically. (Used in the second, the wishing-round).
„Mummy has not scolded me."
„Ah, you want to say that I was friendlier? I am pleased about that!"

„I found it really wonderful that you've hung up the jackets this week."
„Nico did not hit me."
„Aha, you mean he could handle his anger a lot better?" (Friendly correction)
„Yes and I am enthusiastic about how you have learned to use the boxing-bag when you were angry!"
„Daddy, you did not stress me!"
„Aha, you appreciated that I gave you enough time?"
„Dev, you helped with the washing, that made me really pleased!"
„Mohini, you have done your job so well. The jackets in the wardrobe were hung up so neatly."
„Super, how you, Bhasu, have stuck to your revision!"
„Brushing teeth has been really successful. This is wonderful!"
„Yeah, Mummy, you have been telling us brilliant stories that`s why it worked so well!" "Thank you!"
„I thought Wednesday's lunch was great!"
„You have taken time to help me with my homework!"

Round 2 : The **wishing-round**
All express their wishes in a neutral way (not referring to anyone). No nagging or criticising!!! (Fear-centre!)
„My big wish is that on Wednesdays the laundry is put in the basket. This would make it easier for me to do the clothes washing." „I would like the shoes in the entrance hall left neatly, this looks so much nicer."
„I would prefer to be reminded in a friendly way when I have forgotten something." „Actually I don`t want to be reminded because otherwise I won't be able to do it at all!"
„I wish we could make a favourite-menu-plan!"

„I would like more peace and quiet when I do my homework."
„I wish someone would cook my favourite meal!"
„I would appreciate more help in the kitchen."

Round 3 : **Offerings**: every family-member says what he or she can accomplish or contribute.

Round 4 : **Make the list and celebrate**.
A good way is to have a written chores-plan, a to-do-list - hung up with names. But do not let them sign!– This would show your distrust. That which has been done will be mentioned in the next family-meeting; you express your pleasure about it, this is stimulating. In the wishing-round you can wish that it might work better and ask the children what they would need to be more successful.

And then eating a meal together or playing a game without winners or losers.

The feedbacks from the participants in the training sessions that have introduced this 'family activity' into their families are altogether very positive. One mother reported that she was very sceptic as to how her husband might react. However, to her great surprise he was the first to announce his willingness to take charge of the tidiness in the entrance hall upon which the children joined in with enthusiasm: „And I shall clean the kitchen!" „And I am responsible for the cat`s food!" Etc. It was pure joy!

We cannot demand anything anyway. When it is done with threatening, scolding, blaming, punishing and pressure mostly the result is / it ends up with resistance, power-struggles and bad moods. The child will always win no matter how the game ends. It does not work because the age of dictatorship is gone. The best we can do is stay friendly and be firm. Express ourselves in 'yes-sentences':

„Yes, I see you don`t like that so much. In our family we do it like this."
„Everybody does his or her job."

In this way I give the child the security of belonging. Children need the feeling of belonging and the sense of community.
When children do not do their task, their chore: it is better not to mention the child`s name. Stay neutral. No reminding or disapproval because then the child gets (negative) attention – the not-doing has been 'rewarded'! It has to be worthwhile to do the task. At lunch times I tell the children how proud I am of them all that everything is going so well.
So often we forget to give appreciation. (This is not praising: „Oh you are such a good boy/girl! You have been so good!" this is harmful. The child perceives and thinks: I have to be good so that they love me. It is better when the children know what they can *do*, this is clearer than having to 'be good'.)
Praising for nothing is harmful and causes addiction.

Genuine appreciation is recognition of the *work* carried out and makes children strong and proud.

A clear, logical, natural, friendly consequence:
"Unfortunately there is no food, I was not in the mood to do my job either." (Equality).

This sentence might sound really brutal to some parents. Yet when you stay calm and friendly it is only necessary once. Then the children know: same rights for all.

"There are enough carrots and cucumbers, you can make a salad or a dip and munch something."

„Unfortunately the dishes have not been taken out of the dish-washer. As soon as this has happened we can eat."

I ask my son B. (15), who prefers to eat in his room and leaves everything there:

„I have a visitor, maybe you have got a fork?"

As a result he takes all the cutlery and dishes to the kitchen and washes them. This would never have happened in this manner if I had scolded and blamed him!

It helps being aware of our own feelings.

**When I am getting angry
I take a pause from parenting.**

When in an angry state I am really not able to reach them. (It`s useless!)

I wait. I do something for myself.

Take a pause from parenting – just enjoy!

Attention

Sometimes when children feel neglected or have not been given enough attention; they confuse it with 'not-being-loved'.

It can also be a result of spoiling; when we constantly give our time to the children and fulfil their wishes, being bribed by their whining and giving in too often (elastic-band-rules)! Unsuitable attention harms the child. Furthermore parents get more and more irritated and angry because they neglect their own needs.

When you can't ignore bad behaviour, just walk away. For the child it is easier let go of it if you don`t give it any significance stating it every time, naming, blaming or shaming the child.

When we remember instead to use the child's name in calling to them throughout the day, when we talk to, play with and say nice things to them **celebrating their successes** the child won`t need the disruptive behavior so much anymore.

When we need a rest we prepare the child:

„ I'll play with you for 10 more minutes."

Really do it well and give the child all your attention.

"After that I shall lie down for half an hour. You can lie down with me and also have a 'siesta' or play something quietly. What would you like to do?"

Children are very intelligent and creative.
They invent all kinds of games to get our attention.
Also negative attention.

An observation in the kindergarten:
Some boys are always running away from the singing-circle instead of sitting there.

Conventional reaction: the teachers loudly call them by their names. Those boys get much more attention than all the other children who are already sitting in the circle! Now we turn it around: we give attention to all those who are here 'all ready'!

„Most of you are already sitting in the circle! It's great that you are here! The others will certainly join us soon. We 'll reserve some space for them in the meantime."
„They can learn from you, you are such good role models for them!"

Then follows the welcome-song with all their names and a game that everybody loves, or the favourite song of one of the (still missing) boys.

Some teachers tried this out and observed that it did not work out so well in the beginning. However, by the time they became more relaxed in this method the boys came into the circle by themselves. Their self-esteem was strengthened by including them as soon as they were there - 'catching them doing it `right'

„Great that you are here. Britta wanted the witches song. What is your favourite song? The five fishes? Oh yes, the other children also like that, right? We shall sing it right after this one. I am looking forward to it!"

The running away will stop as soon as they do not get the attention any more. Yet if they have an urge to move their body they must be allowed to let the energy out. As soon as something interests, fascinates or thrills them they will sit down by themselves.

Hanging onto the apron strings

„This child is constantly at my side. I cannot even go to the loo alone!" many mothers complain.

What helps are the following sentences:
"Yes you want to be very close to me. Come here, hold on to me very tightly and stay with me. Don`t leave me, I want you to come with me wherever I go, even to the toilet."

You could even turn 'clinging' into a joyful play!

Now maybe you think as a logical conclusion
that the child will cling to you even more.
As we function *psycho*logically that`s why exactly the opposite will occur if you really mean what you say because it will give the child a feeling of security. So being authentic as much as possible is worth it.
We can practise that as well.

Getting Up in the Morning

A mother, Debbie, has difficulties with structure, time and keeping to appointments! She`d prefer to live spontaneously. Now she is challenged with the needs of her four year old daughter Isis. The security that she needs: with managing time, applying a daily structure and keeping to diary!

Debbie recounts: „Since we get up a quarter of an hour earlier, everything works out much better. We have less stress. The children have an alarm-clock and take responsibility. Since I have introduced the clock it works. Isis knows the schedule; we have been drawing it and hung it up.

She is running here and there checking. "Sasha", she says to her younger brother who is enjoying all this very much, "look we have brushed our teeth, now it`s time for the shoes. Then the jacket, the bag ... and so on."

Isis loves to linger around. She is suffering from the pressure of time. She has to meet up with a small group of children who come to escort her. If she goes out too late, they are gone. But she loves meeting up with them.

An 'integrative' father in the group makes the suggestion to introduce a 'go slow-day'. Debbie is fine with this idea and wants to try it out!

Introduction of the time-table and the clock:

„Now you are old enough to be responsible. Daddy and I are giving you an alarm-clock so you can get up all by yourselves from next week. We shall practise this."

„I am sure you will be able to do it."
„I am proud that you are now so big and responsible."
These sentences show your genuine, honest validation, appreciation, and trust.

Enthusiastic valuation and appreciation in this face, too!

Needs

We all have our needs but how to get them all under one hat? We have to have more than one hat, then it is easier.
First it is my turn: what do I need? How can I recharge my batteries? What cheers me up? What do I like to do?
Then the partner: what do we want to do together? What do we both enjoy? What recharges our batteries? Where and when should this happen?
And then come the children!
Then we can give them quality attention and meet their needs more adequately.
Especially the mothers - I tell them repeatedly: create little islands in your everyday life! Identifying your limits is important. This helps.

„Now it is my siesta and I don`t want to be disturbed for half an hour. After that I am there for you again." (Showing the clock)

„Dad and mum are going out on their own tonight. The sitter (Not 'babysitter', as the children are not babies anymore! Best you tell the name of the person.) will play with you.
We are looking forward to coming back and seeing you asleep in your beds. You know you look so sweet then, like angels. Tomorrow we can all go to the zoo (beach, pool etc.) together."

„At 9 pm it`s leisure time for us (parents). We want to be on our own. You can stay in your room, or in your beds and read a little bit.

*Tomorrow we can talk about it all. There is no hurry.
I wish you a good night!"*
*„You can build something out of sand. I am reading my
book now. Afterwards I shall come and see you.
You can show me what you have built."*

"Daddy? You come and play with me?"
"Yes! 'Our special time' ('quality-time') - just for the two of us."

You can take it for your own relaxation!

Orders, Commands

Since our form of government is not a dictatorship led by a dictator (reflected in families of that time with the head of family as the authority) this commanding approach to children does not work anymore. Children are less afraid and show resistance. When a child has heard too many orders it will develop disorders to express its needs for self-determination.

It is more effective to present our wishes instead of giving commands; or to introduce clear rules that everybody has to hold on to and obey. (See "Rules" ... 130)

Warning! If we disguise our orders with begging and wishing the child will not engage. Children want to decide for themselves whether to please their parents. So this approach annoys them because they have no real opportunity for a choice. If we wish and ask we should be able to expect and accept a 'no' as well.

If nobody has signed up to the household chore list:
„I`d love somebody to help me with the evening washing up. Who of you could assist me?"
If no child is offering its help the partner should do so and be a role-model for them. But later we should deny them a wish by stating we don't want to either; yet without naming the reason or getting angry!
If we are annoyed and want to pay them back it will end up in a power-struggle. If we stay calm it is felt as a friendly consequence and therefore will be more effective. The child might be frustrated too but through our calm behaviour it is learning that there are equal rights for all and that its not-helping can have consequences.

But then it can decide itself if it wants to help next time. Then this will happen out of free will.

„You want me to help you with your home-work? Sorry, I just don`t fancy that right now!"
„In our family we do it like this - so our 'community' works much better for everyone. We also need your help."
„What do you need?"
„What would help you to get your chores finished?"

Bearing the 'Not-doing'!
(Mine and his):

When one of my sons refused to do his job which was to take down the rubbish-bags for weeks I put each bag back into his room. Shall it smell there! It did not help. I became more and more annoyed and angry.
The solution: my boyfriend at that time took the bags down and said to B. in a friendly way afterwards:

„I realised that you did not have time to do your job. I took the bags down for you."

B. thanked him embarrassed. From then on the rubbish-bags where no issue any more.
Fortunately I could control myself; my boy-friend had been a generous, friendly model.

And if my child demands:
"You must do this and this!" I ask myself where he/she has learned this.
And I always say to the children:
"I decide for myself. And you for yourself!"
By the way, this is also a good way to prevent abuse.

Bed-Wetting

There are different reasons for bed-wetting; most of the times it has to do with tension and fear.
Basically this helps: relaxing and making no fuss about it, no scolding, no blaming, no punishing – this would only increase the fear.
Maybe clarify with a doctor.

Be relaxed:

„It does not matter, this can happen. No problem, we can change the bed together."
„In the time being you can sleep without diapers for sure."
To the son: „You can help me water the garden with the hose!" Let him play fire-brigade!
Substitute! Making a fire and put it out by peeing over it. For girls also!
Give them warmth, affection, and a feeling of safety during the day.
It happened that a bed-wetting child (during a therapy) suddenly became cheeky; this points to the fact that it was getting more courageous.
(If it is too much: see 'Swearing' ... 97)
Now we can encourage them even more and show him or her how to use their newly found power usefully.

The stronger the child becomes
and the more they can show their feelings / emotions
the less they will need the bed-wetting any more.

Play 'Boss'

Max said that he was the 'boss'. The mother then answered: „No, Max, I am the boss!" Then he threw something, he was frustrated. She was angry.
Somebody made a suggestion: How would it be to let him be the chief for a while?
Oh yes, maybe with a captain`s cap, using the clock, showing him the time?
Yes, the mother had not seen it like this before.
She thought she had always to be above him, having the last say. This she has of course. It is a play. He also wants to ... She decides to try it out.
Later the mother tells us that surprisingly nothing 'bad' had happened! She had noticed how pleasurable it had been for him, he did not 'take advantage' of it.
(There are only imaginings, expectations and fears about what could happen!)

„Yes I hear, you like to be boss. That`s fun!"
„Yes, you can be the boss. We shall take turns. I 'll show you with the clock for how long and then we will change over."
„Every child can be the boss for 5 minutes and then chose the new boss. I am looking forward to this. For sure it`s gonna be exciting!"
In the group: every day a new boss is chosen.
Helpful book: 'Where the Wild Things Are' by Maurice Sendak, Harper & Row. Every child can be a Max giving orders. The 'others' are the 'Wild Things' (or monsters) that obey him, they do what he is telling them to do. When he says 'Stop!' everybody stops and waits for the election of the new king or queen.
The children love this play because it is so fair.

Jealousy (Fear of Loss)

Jealousy is quite an ordinary feeling, it is based in the fear of losing somebody or somebody`s love. With its actions the jealous child shows its vulnerability, its helplessness, its disappointment. If we are interested in the child's emotions, ask how it feels and when we acknowledge them, we take the fear out of the child, it feels safe and accepted.

„*Are you sad?"*
„*Are you angry?"*
„*Yes, this is very unpleasant."*
„*Do you sometimes think we do not love you as much as before?"*
„*Would you like to have mum and dad all for yourself?"*
„*Now every day we shall have 'our time' (or our 'special time', 'quality time') only the two of us!"*

5-10 minutes a day can create miracles! Showing the time on the clock so the child knows when the time is over.
„*What would you like to do with me? Your wish. You can choose. Would you like to look at a book together? Draw something?"*
„*In the evening the two of us will take a bath together. Then we can play ships. I am looking forward to that!"*
(Splash, play, have fun!)
„*We'll look at your baby-album. Look, this is what you looked like when you were a new-born!"*

Tell him or her about this wonderful time. Build up trust and safety by the day, and letting the child 'play baby'.

The older child should benefit from being older. For example in bed at night having the light on for 10 minutes longer. It needs more attention and notice. Letting them help and giving appreciation creates miracles and strengthens the self-esteem:

„I am so proud of you! I don`t know what I would do without you! You really help me so much!
I am so glad you are my big son / daughter! I am so glad you are here!"

Addressing the feelings of older children, taking some time, being really, honestly, interested in their world will help generate a better relationship with them. Instead of rejecting their movies, videos, idols and games on principle it is better to wonder what they are, letting them show you, explain to you, taking part in the game:

„How does this actually work in this game? What is it that we need? What skills? Would you like to show me? I`d love to see it. I have some time right now."

„Do you feel unfairly treated? What would help you (to feel better)? I would love to spend some time with you. Would you like to go for a bike-ride with me?"

„We could go shopping together? I would love to have tea with you afterwards. Would you fancy that?"

Going Shopping

Good preparation goes a long way!
Make a menu-plan for the whole week *with* the family.
Let the children make the list of what has to be bought.
Shop from the list. Plan in a good deal of time,
including the journey to and from the shop,
supermarket or market. The children will be able to
look for certain products in a super-market.
They can look for the items on the list and bring them
to you. Watch out: no competition or rivalry!

Emphasise the 'togetherness' and helping each other!

„I wonder if you can find the whole-wheat-noodles together! They are always so difficult to find!"
Give appreciation.
„It is so lovely that you can now help each other!"
„What is it you would like to look for first?"
„Great! I am so grateful for your help! Now, what comes next?" (Practise reading!)

If there is any whining about sweets you can say:

„Oh yes, you would like some chocolate? I am sorry we don`t have it on the list! Can you remember to write it down next time?"
„At the cash desk they have displayed sweets on purpose so that we buy them! But we won`t be conned!"

The reaction of the children at the next shopping trip:
„Right, we won`t buy this, mum! We are not so stupid!"

Saying Sorry

Many grown-ups think that the child has to apologise and they demand it or force it from them. This is absolute nonsense and on top of that it is humiliating. The child can only feel sorry (contrite) from real discernment. When the child feels sincerely sorry then true reconciliation and healing can occur.
The children should be able to find the empathy in their own hearts to feel sorry.
Being made to say sorry evokes hatred to the other, which is then reinforced.
We always presume the innocence of the child which makes it easier for them to admit the mistake - they are ashamed anyway. Some children hide their shame behind laughter or unconcern so as not to feel or show their own vulnerability. Let`s not be hoodwinked by that but let`s help them by saying:

„I am sure you did not really want to hurt him/her so badly on purpose!"
„You must have been very angry!"
„Are you hurt?"
„Do you feel treated unfairly?"
„What can you do to make this up? You have an idea?"

Then they are much more willing to approach the other/s.
We can be role models for them. When they frequently hear us say:

„I am sorry, I did not want this to happen ...!", they also can say more easily: *„I am sorry. "*

I composed a song with some of the miracle-sentences in it which promotes reconciliation and contains the recipe for making peace.

Children should not be forced to say sorry – it is much more beautiful, harmonious and authentic when they look into the tear-smeared face of their companion and can say heartily:

„I am sorry. I did not want to hurt you!"

Or when a child can say, that it has been made angry. We don`t ask who had started it because this separates the children even more into victim and aggressor. We address the feelings (in the form of a question):

„Are you sad?"
Both of them are mostly angry, sad or both.
We ask:
„What do you need?"
After I introduced the following song into my music-lessons I noticed how much easier and faster the children could reconcile with each other and afterwards be better participants in the lesson. The reminder to not quarrel or hit each other was never used again and so we were all much better off!

I am sorry-song
"I am sorry, because of
what happened on the playground just now,
I really am!
I was angry, and I hurt you,
and on top of that I said something really bad.
Are you still sad?---(wait)---Are you still angry?--- (wait)---
What do you need to laugh happily again?

(In my experience at this point both of them are already laughing in recognition).

I would like to shake hands, be friends,
and would like to make peace - now!"

After this 'now' the children invent signs of peace with their hands (maybe feet). When they have made the signs they can dance freely together to the melody of the song with la la la. So... just be free and courageous. Invent a melody or borrow one from another song ...

Bhasu and Dev on a rocking-horse together

Encouragement

It`s about giving validation and appreciation.
Letting experiences of success happen.
It is like a miracle to see what encouraging instead of criticising does to children!
Encouragement makes children strong and self-assured, boosts their self-esteem and self-confidence. Strong children don`t have the need to develop so many disorders, they are proud and content.

Loreena has overcome some fears

„Hey, super, you have made it!"
„All on your own! Great!"
„Fantastic!"
„Congratulations!"
„Great how you did it!"
"In spite of your fear! Super!"

Enlarge the successes:

"Today you have already ..."
"I am so proud of you!"
"I do not know what I would do without you!"

Make them feel at ease, give confidence:

"It's easy, just like this!"
"We are practising. You will see, every day it will work out better!" "You are just perfect as you are!"
"Adults also make mistakes!"
"Perfect is boring!"
"You`ll make it for sure!"

In one kindergarten there was a rather high climbing-tower with a platform in the middle of the sand-box. The children could climb up and climb or slide down all by themselves. The teachers did not help or interfere. If the children wanted to be lifted up, the teachers would say firmly and friendly:

"In our kindergarten (using the 'we-language' for an inclusive-feeling) *all children climb up by themselves; this will make you strong. You can practise every day, and you will see that you will get better and better every time you try! I am sure that you will succeed! Your muscles are getting stronger and stronger!"*
(Giving trust in advance).

Or the teachers would exaggerate with humour, acting out:
"But think, if we had to lift all the children up the whole day! Ohhhh, my poor back! I cannot do this!"

Sometimes the children got hold of some parents that helped them up. Then the teachers would look away on purpose or pretend to be very astonished when the child shouted down from above: „Look where I am! I am up here!"
„Great! You made it! How did you do it?"
„Aha, very clever! You found someone to lift you up!"

Of course when a child wants to jump into your arms from up there – no problem! You can catch them with wide open arms! This is not the same as lifting them down. Most of the time it is ourselves who are afraid that the child might fall down. Where it has got up on its own it can come down alone as well. When as a small child it has been allowed to fall it has been learning this and will not hurt itself so much as if we had protected it and kept the child safe all the time from everything.
Which we cannot do, anyway.

Yes, sometimes we would love to put our children onto such a 'protection-island' ...!

Food, Meals and Table-Manners

Nino is enjoying his pasta!

Meals should be joyful and tasty.
Whosoever eats relaxed has a better digestion!
It is better to discuss issues before or after meals, not at the dining-table.

„We can discuss this after lunch, when I can give you the time! Is that ok with you?"
„We can talk it over right now, and when we have finished and found a solution we can start eating."
„Mummy(Daddy) has been cooking so brilliantly again today! Thank you so much! Lovely!"
„I am glad you like it!"
The child should be able to choose from **a great variety** of food.
It is unhealthy to force the child to try (taste) food. The body itself knows best what`s good for it. What we do is provide numerous choices of abundance.

A girl once told me that her mother was always decorating her plate by laying mandalas of fruits and vegetables. Only then would she eat.

When my children were young I used to cut up fruit and vegetables and have them in my bag. My children picked out what they liked, coming and going during their play.

The word 'healthy' should not be mentioned! The children should eat what they like, not because it is 'healthy'.

We are models for the children and eat with **pleasure and joy:**

„Oh how I love this! It tastes so wonderful! And on top of all I love all these great vitamins in it!"

We buy healthy food which we like to eat ourselves as well. At home we make a shopping-list together with the children which we stick to strictly during shopping.

„I am very sorry, there are no biscuits on the list. Can you think of this next time? Then we shall write it down."

We **wait** together:
*„Yes, I am also very hungry. Can you **bear it** for ten minutes more with me?"*

Dessert is frequently used to force the children to empty their plates. This is very harmful because through this the children lose their original instinctive feeling for their body.

They eat although they don`t like it or are not hungry anymore and may develop eating-disorders later.

Pressure and force, constant offering and feeding after or between meals can ruin healthy eating-behaviour.

To feel really hungry is much healthier than feeling stuffed.

It is advantageous to digestion to separate dessert from lunch. It can be pushed to the afternoon and be named more accurately as to what it is. We can also dispose of sweets that are stuffed with industrial sugar and instead of this create delicious tasty desserts out of fruits, berries, nuts and dried fruits. Best together with the children – they love it!

„For snack-time we shall eat mango-pieces."
„We shall make a tasty strawberry-cheese- cream together!"
„We can make a yummy Birchermuesli. What do we need for that?"

Eating-disorders are loud cries for help that must be taken seriously. Very often, behind them lie psychological problems that have to be thoroughly examined. Here I recommend by all means therapy with a competent expert whom you trust and with whom your child feels safe and at ease. Best would be a systemic therapy where the whole family is included - otherwise only the symptoms will be addressed. Deep healing and change can only happen when all involved help together and the family member can be re-integrated back into the family circle.

Not getting enough may be expressed as a feeling of need, the sensation of deficiency. I have experienced this with children whose parents follow a particular lifestyle with regard to nutrition and want the child to eat the same as they do.

One child`s reaction was defiance: after every snack between meals, outside the family home this child began to scream and shout as soon as the fruit or piece of cracker had been eaten. „More! I want more!" This only happened when the parents were in public with their child. At home or when there was no audience this did not happen.

Parents can try different things to prepare for the 'tantrum'.

They could **react differently from usual**. For example: take extra pieces of fruit and offer more instantly before the child demands more:

*„Well it's great(!) that you have such an appetite! **Luckily** we have **enough to eat** with us!"* (Calming, relaxing!)

„Yes, I know, you would love to have a second ice-cream. Yes, that was very tasty! Tomorrow you can have another one."

„Yes, I see, this makes you sad and angry, right? Yes, let your feelings out."

Children that eat less are less hungry!

If we let them help with the cutting and peeling they can nibble from the raw vegetables. Usually children love to eat what they have prepared themselves. It can also be more fun having meals together with other children! A nutrition-specialist told me that we have enough from one hand-full at a meal!

No pressure! No offering all the time as this arouses resistance. Trust. Reduce the tension. The child's body is probably getting everything it needs out of whatever it is eating anyway! – This is a very good exercise.

And remember: no child starves from free will!

Playing with food is allowed because it is a pleasurable experience. We could practise Geography. (For example with the mashed potatoes and the sauce.)

„Aha, is this Etna or Vesuvius? Is this the lava coming out on top? What`s the name of the biggest river in …? Do you know it?"

Or giving them riddles or rhymes:
Riddles make the children much cleverer because the brain is stimulated when they have to think for themselves instead of being told the answer:

*„Where does the cucumber-crocodile swim?
Maybe in the …?"*

Or translate into other languages:
„Would you like another sweet potato, sweetie?"
„Möchtest du noch eine Süsskartoffel, du Süsser?"

Throwing food means that the child is full and should be allowed to leave the table. Remove its plate.

„Aha I see you do not want to eat any more. You can go and play."
Table-manners:
Incorporate eating 'nicely' and 'ghastly' into a play:

„Aha, I see you want to devour everything with your fingers today. We can have a pirate`s meal tomorrow (today?) On Wednesday I will invite you to the king`s table and then we shall dine like princes and princesses with knives and forks."

Looks like a pirates`meal with 'the pirates of Patnem, Goa'

Emptying the water-glass

„You are not thirsty?"
„I see you have finished."

Put away the glass firmly (without talking.) Next time you put in only a little water. Let the child do a lot of scooping and ladling, emptying and watering in play. Give them the joyous message:

„This afternoon you can play water-games in the sand-box again."

Here a nice episode of an integrative mother, Ines:

Ines`s sister Britta is visiting for lunch. They are talking. Ines`s two year old daughter is emptying the water-cup over her T-shirt. Ines is calmly carrying on as before talking to her sister **neglecting the non-desired behaviour** of her daughter. (Thus the child experiences what`s happening. It is not so bad anyway.)
Britta sees what is happening and holds herself back.

(She would love to jump forward and snatch the water-cup and say something ...)
After a while the child says: „Mummy, wet!"
Ines, in a friendly way (not scolding, not teaching!) says:

"Yes, when you empty the water on your T-shirt it gets wet." (Short break.) *„Would you like to change?"*

Ines lifts her daughter from the chair and calmly goes to another room to change her. Britta is amazed, is affected by what she has witnessed and wants to be and act like this in future.
What would have been different if she had scolded? The relationship! The T-Shirt was wet already and now the child knows what the consequences are.

Nobody is forced to try.
Otherwise the child forgets (unlearns) to listen to its belly-sensation. No child starves out of free will. Waiting for the next meal makes them strong and prevents addiction. A little hunger is much healthier then over-eating.
In between we can offer raw-food, fruits and vegetables that can be cut by the children (two year olds can already cut with rounded knives, older ones with pointed ones.) They have to be sharp! To cut oneself once makes them proud. I always say in the beginning:

„It does not matter if somebody cuts himself, this can happen. I have enough band-aid with me."
This is calming. The children cut themselves less because they concentrate much better (without fear).

Make a **menu-plan** with the family. Every family member should get their own favourite meal 1-2 times a week that everyone eats as well. Whoever does not eat at lunch waits until snack-time at 4p.m when there will be fruit or vegetables offered. The left-overs from lunch can be warmed up at dinner and offered again. Who does not like it can have raw-food again.
Firmly and calmly:

„When you say 'yucky!' it hurts me. In our family we say: I don`t like this."

„I am sorry that you don`t fancy daddy's favourite meal much."

„On Wednesday it is your favourite menu. I am already looking forward to it!"

Table-Manners
TABOO-SENTENCES are better to be dropped because they spoil the atmosphere at the table:

No singing whilst eating!
No talking during eating!
No talking with your mouth full!

Let`s use the 'we'-language instead of demanding or prohibiting:

„It`s nice that you like to sing! I love this song, too! When we eat we need our mouths for chewing. That`s why in our family we sing before and after meals. This works much better!"

„We can talk after swallowing. Then we can hear and understand each other much better!"

Simon is throwing plates. What is the situation? Grandmother is putting too many things on the table and Simon gets too many instructions. There are too many stimulations. The adults talk to each other in lots of short sentences as they prepare the table and it feels hectic.

Simon is totally exhausted and feels left out.

The grown-ups should talk less and more calmly and most of all *to* him not about him over his head. To let him help with setting the table would strengthen his feeling of self-worth. Then he would not need to disrupt them so much.

The next time she is trying out something new:
The mother gives attention and appreciation when he shows the desired behaviour.
She tries to ignore the 'disturbing' conduct of her son.

Simon is sitting at the table, takes his table-mat, looks at the mother and drops it on the floor.

She does not react. Result: it does not happen any more because it is not worth it any more. It worked! Giving no attention, not noticing: that`s new! Before she used to always teach and 'train' him. But Simon knows already very well what his mother wants.

Usually children know what we want from them. If we do not remind them constantly it is easier for them to behave the desired way ...

Last words to 'food and table-manners':
offer a great, healthy variety
and then just
relax and enjoy!

Swearing, Being Cheeky (Impudent)

It is a given: to swear sometimes feels really good, doesn`t it? With this we can let out bottled up adrenaline. It is important to notice what language, what words we are using ourselves. Often children come home with swear-words. They have picked them up somewhere and are trying them out for effect. When they get a lot of attention, also negative attention, it will be worth it to carry on. With very young children we can just 'turn a deaf ear' to it and pretend to know nothing about what they are saying, or ask them what it means. (Usually they don`t even know the meaning.)

What works very well with pre-school children and children up to about 10 years old is the remark that we don`t swear in our family and that they can say or (even better!) scream the 'ugly words' into the rubbish-bin, paper-basket or toilet. It is good to talk about this beforehand and agree to it together.

At the camp I had a compost-bucket for this purpose. As soon as one of us said for example 'shit' the others shouted: "Compost!", which gave the whole situation a humorous element.

Repeatedly I get very positive feedbacks. Family members find the 'swearing into the bucket' very pleasurable.

We don`t have to swallow anything down!
Out with the sh..! But yes: with guidance.

Another possibility is to invent our own bad words. I did this spontaneously with some kids and all ended up with hilarious laughter.

You want some examples: you crumbled biscuit, you mouldy old dough, you squashed potato, you rotten lazybone, you crashed stinky egg, you old shrinked garden-hose …

In the music-school I had to firmly hold the rubbish-bag and shake it so that all the 'bad words' could jumble up and get confused – an idea from the children.

„Aha, I hear you are angry: here is the bin, please swear into that."

„Is that all? You do not know any other words? I want every little bit in here! They must all come out!"

„In our family we do not swear. If you have to let it out, into the bin or toilet with it!"

*„What do you say?
Grandpa is swearing? Well, I presume he does not know about the swearing-bin yet."*

„Yes, sometimes grown-ups swear when they are angry."

With teenagers:
„I hear that you are fed up." (Better not mention the feelings, they cannot stand it. Teenagers are very vulnerable and sensitive and prefer to approach issues on a more factual level.

„It hurts me when you use these words."
„And what does this mean now exactly?" (Yes, dare to inquire when they are using slang or 'foreign' words.)
„In our family we talk differently, I find this language hurting." (Sexist, discriminating, racist.)

When children call you 'silly mummy' or 'silly cow' you can say depending on your mood „Mouuuuuh!"

Or not reacting at the moment but later on:
"You would like me to read to you? Sorry, a silly cow does not read."
Or ask them right back: „Are you angry?"
When the child puts out its tongue you can put out your tongue as well making a 'competition' out of it.

**(= Using the energy instead of rejecting it:
Judo instead of Boxing!)**

„Wow, you certainly do have a long tongue! Can you reach your nose? Your chin? I have to try this too!"
„At the doctors we must also put out our tongue a long way and say 'UUUUUhhh'. Let`s practise this just now!"
With an older child:
„Ah, that`s interesting! Show me again!"
Or join in the play. It feels good!

Tongue-out-selfies before bed-time

Demanding, Overstraining, Patronising or Promoting

Many parents want to cultivate the best in their children (encourage learning) but sometimes this ends up in overstraining, demanding or patronising. Some parents make their children learn musical instruments even though they do not want to: this is a compensation of their own not fulfilled wishes.
There was one family I was coaching whose three-year-old child regressed deeply after the birth of the second sibling and presented with autistic tendencies.
This child was babbling, tottering around, isolating itself in play and wanting to be a baby again. The father was terribly afraid it might not develop 'appropriately' and had been searching for an acceptable university for his child at that time. He was completely overburdening the child. Every play activity became a training / teaching session; every 'inadequate behaviour' was punished by locking the child up in its room. It was rewarded, punished, threatened, bribed and given promises – of course nothing worked.
Only in fresh and inventive family play ('Original Play') and with coaching on mats (where we did this, too) could the child relax by rolling around with its parents who understood then that it was more helpful to let the child be a child. **A child chooses by itself what it wants to play and therefore nourishes itself with its curiosity and interest.**
How to promote without overstraining
When we observe the child, when we give it the largest possible space in a natural surrounding it will show us what it is interested in. One mother was complaining that her child was only "messing around with the

beautiful newly bought water colours" and was "only mixing the colours till everything was brown". What an excellent experience! It is learning what happens when colours are mixed! It is great fun smearing, paddling about, splashing. This is fitting to the age. Finger colours would be more appropriate or clay/ mud. The mother can paint with the water colours herself in the way she would like to.

We can have things available to be used by the child when we are doing activities that we enjoy. Maybe it would then awaken in our children the desire to do the same. It will develop by itself when we allow it.

In the parent-child-singing sessions or other courses for young children it is most important that parents like to do it; then the child will be able to follow and have fun. It is best to invite the children to join in and then let them decide for themselves.

Like us children want to choose for themselves and not be directed by others.

„You don`t have to. You can simply be here and enjoy. You can join in any time anywhere."

„The door stays shut. You can leave as soon as we have sung the good-bye-song."

(Set your limits firmly and friendly.)

„You can eat and drink before and after the lesson, also the dummy / pacifier stays outside, we don`t need this when singing, you are all grown up now!"

(Setting borders and making them proud.)

„Yes it is okay if you are just watching."

„Yes you can run around in a circle, energy has to (wants to) be allowed out!"

„Now we shall soon be dancing. Or would you prefer to play horses instead?" (Giving them a choice.)

Offer things for free play (do not make suggestions):

"Here we have coloured letters and numbers. What can we do with them?"
Just let them 'work'. They might build towers or houses or sort them in colours or forms or size.

> **Much inspiration can always be found outdoors in nature in any weather and every season.**

Playing with autumn-leaves
on a playground in Bern, Switzerland

Feelings, Emotions
(Anger, Rage, Fear, Joy, Sadness)

1. All feelings are valid.
2. All feelings are important – they show us when something is 'wrong'. When it feels comfortable we want to stay.

Unpleasant feelings make us either change the situation or want to change it.

When children are making problems they show us that they have a problem. They need our help.

The words of one of my songs show different feelings. Adults and children are usually moved by it. You can invent a melody, make a similar song or read it as a poem and talk about it.

'Feelings are important'
1. Are you sad or are you angry,
Do you just wanna be alone?
Showing tears or showing teeth
Or just wanting to be on your own?

Refrain:
Please tell me how you feel,
Please tell me what you need!
Your feelings are alright, all feelings are important,
I love you just the way you are right now!

2. Are you envious, are you grumpy,
Feeling like you wanna punch my nose?
Are you feeling down and miserable,
Nobody presenting you a rose?
Ref.: Please tell me ...

3. Are you frightened, feeling insecure,
Want to hide beneath the bed?
You feel abandoned, a total failure
No one sharing their bread?
Ref.: Please tell me ...

4. Are you happy, are you joyful,
Something wonderful happened today?
Feel the pleasure and feel excitement,
Like on a journey, flying away?

Ref.: So share your feelings with me,
I like to feel with you!
All these many emotions
Like so many bright colours,
Together they make a rainbow,
As beautiful as you!
Through rain and through sun
It makes this many colours,
From heaven down to earth,
Just as beautiful as you! (A. H.)

For more profoundness: The Integrative Dealing with Feelings ... 33

Limits and My Own Experience With Limits

Children need the widest possible freedom inside clear limits. These we defend clearly and friendly:

„These are our (family) rules."
(see also 'Rules' ... 130)
„We do it like that."
„I want the wall to stay clean. You can paint here."
„Ouch, this hurts. We caress. You can hit the cushion."
„We have lunch from 12 to 1 o`clock, after that we clean the table. The next meal will be at 4 p.m."

A little story on the side:
after more than fifteen years of experience and work with the integrative method with children and teaching parents I thought I had the know-how.
In any case with the young ones. But this summer a five year old taught me that we never finish learning! Life presents us again and again challenging situations where we have to look anew – luckily!
I had worked a lot; I was tired and tidying up outside. Sanna wanted to play with me; she did not want me to tidy up but wanted my attention.
She was running after me, went into my way, making the clown, making fun of me. As she started to pull my clothes and went into my way again I started to get loud! (Me, that teaches people parenting without scolding and punishing!)
„Sanna, this is enough! Stop it!", it came out of my mouth. In this moment I realised how irritated I was and could respond to her (and my) behaviour:

"Sorry, I have gotten loud! Yes, you would like me to play with you. And I did not listen, this made you angry, right? And then I got angry myself. Okay: the faster I can tidy up here the earlier we can sit down together and play something. Do you help me?"

She did not help me but she let me finish: this was possible because I had noticed her, spoken honestly and friendly to her and taken her seriously. But I had also taken myself and my needs seriously.
Sanna gave me the opportunity to become aware of myself and my feelings that I otherwise had ignored and covered with this continually ongoing activity. Other way round: the body was tired, the nervous system irritated, actually I did not even want to tidy up but rest! I had come to my own limits.

If we take the `disturbances` of the children as a chance to be aware of ourselves and to get to know ourselves better, then all of us can profit.

Homework

Kindergarten child Loreena loves to play 'homework'

If teachers taught all their 'homework' at school, which would mean they had reached their goals, the children would have free time after school! If children could learn through topic-oriented work and with their interests, they would explore and find out together: putting on presentations and learning from each other. They would work with pleasure and dedication and even carry on at home voluntarily because they like it so much. Well…. your child goes to an ordinary government school and has homework to do. How can you help? How can you behave for the best outcome? Never make the teacher 'the bad one' (the child neither, of-course! It is nobody`s 'fault'.)
When the teacher has scolded or given extra work as a punishment, rather enquire:

"What do you think the teacher wants you to achieve with this?"
"It is great that you have so much homework, you will become so clever!"
"Where do you want to start?"
"I am sitting on the sofa and reading. You can call me if you need any help."
"First you can play outdoors for an hour. After that the studying will be much easier."
"Everything you manage alone will make you more intelligent!"
"Can you ask that tomorrow at school? I don`t know myself what the teacher meant by that."
"Could you explain this to me? What exactly is it that you don`t understand?"
"How could we start? Do you have any ideas?"
"Great! Now you can practise right handwriting as well as left hand! That will be a great advantage!"

When the children explain their homework to us, they sometimes find out by themselves how to do it, what is meant by the instructions. Give the responsibility back to the children.

Homework is an issue between the teacher and the child. If the teacher is expecting you to help you can say that you do your best (relaxing him / her), and then 'integratively' encourage and strengthen your child at home.

Helping

The most important thing is to let them help out when they are very young because they want to! They want to be a part of the community, contributing their share, wanting to feel useful. If they are hearing when very young: „No, you cannot do this! Let me do it for you! You are too small for that. You are too slow (clumsy)!" they are discouraged, frustrated and give up. Later the child probably does not want to help anymore!

Loreena, 1 year and 8 months, is helping proudly to set the table, carrying real porcelain-plates

In Rudolf Dreikurs` and Vicky Soltz`s book 'The Challenge of Parenthood' we find wonderful examples. Five-year old Elsie was happily busy changing her bed. She drew the blanket to and fro until finally she had it as she wanted. The mother came into the room, saw the 'not perfectly made' bed and said:

„I shall make the bed myself, darling, those blankets are too heavy for you." With this the mother not only showed Elsie her inferiority but also her own superiority by skillfully putting the blanket in order while Elsie stood watching downhearted ... Soon Elsie will have the feeling: „What`s the use of it? Mummy can do it so much better."

What discouragement! Elsie has lost the pleasure in helping and doing something herself. She believes what her mother implied: I am too small, too weak ...
The mother could have reacted completely differently! She could have shown her **joy** over the **efforts** and the **good will** of her daughter:

„How lovely that you have pulled up the blanket!" or „Look, my big girl is changing her own bed!"

………… After letting her change the bed alone, the mother could encourage her by skillfully made remarks (in the form of questions):

„What do you think would happen, if you rolled back all the blankets together and pulled them up at the same time?"
The mother could suggest changing the bed together:
„Would you like to change the whole bed with me? I find it a great help and what a helper I have in you!"
„So ... we take the side of the mattress and slide a piece of the sheet underneath ... now how are you doing sir / madam-head-of-the-bed now?"
This way learning becomes pleasurable play. And the relationship becomes really more pleasant, too.

Faced with the motherly, sometimes fatherly perfectionism children can quickly and easily be discouraged and give up.

What they need is repeated encouragement, appreciation and validation. Praise for the action, but this in moderation and never for the person. "You are such a good girl!" is harmful because the child just wants to be 'nice only in order to please parents and this suppresses other feelings.

Appreciation:

„You have managed so well already!"

We take no notice of the 'not yet perfect' and rather direct our attention to the effort of the child, its good intentions:

„I can see how much effort you put in! You really have a lot of staying power!"

When the child is dissatisfied with itself:

„This does not matter! You will see, you will get better and better. For me this is fine. I really find it quite wonderful!"

Behind this there is the encouraging message: You are just fine! You are good enough!

„Fantastic, how you did that!"

„You really do help me! I don`t know what I would do without you!"

At two years old, Loreena washed the salad leaves and took them to her mother; put the porcelain-plates on the table and the cushions on the chairs. Her face was red with effort, pride and joy. At three years old she was cutting the vegetables with a sharp, pointed knife and collecting herbs from the garden, knowing all the names!

On the next page Loreena is helping me make a salad, she scrapes an Avocado and cuts vegetables

After the parent/child singing sessions Matteo prefers to stay with me and helps me clean the room.
He does this thoroughly and with dedication.

In the International Kindergarten „Vrindhavan" in Patnem, Goa, India, where I have often team taught and coached, the self-reliance of the children is promoted. For example: each child clears away its own plate and cutlery after the meal. Nobody is forced to eat up (finish) their meal. The children scrape the leftovers into a bowl for the dogs. Plates and spoons are put into another container. This happens without direction from the adults, and it works with great success!

On the following page Loreena, 4 yrs. 8mths. and her brother Nepomuk, 2 ½ yrs. are working with me in the garden.

We can see how glad and proud he is that he can help us.
So he freely expresses his joy!

Telling Tales, Complaining

In a music-school-class the girls were always coming to me telling tales: „Missis Huber, the boys are teasing us! You have to tell them to stop!"
They were used to getting help from their teacher who always scolded the boys after the girls` complaint.
I told the girls something different:

„Hm. Yes, this is really annoying, isn`t it? What would you like to tell them?"
„No, you have to tell them!"
„Oh, you know, when you tell them yourself, it is much more effective! In my classes the children always tell each other what they find annoying. This makes you strong. You can do it, I am sure!"

They were not used to a reaction like this, were surprised, and after standing around for a little bit set off. They ran to the boys: „Hey, stop this messing around now!" From now on they do not come to ask for help anymore and solve their problems by themselves. The boys are really impressed and listen to them.

It is good to listen to children, react to their feelings, and not give any attention to the 'victimiser' who is somewhere else (here an example with a younger kid):
„Uwe has hit me!"
„Oh yes, this hurts!" „Shall I blow on it? Caress?"
„Uwe is stupid!"
„Are you angry?"
„He is always arguing!"
„Oh yes, I know, this feels very unpleasant!"

When both are running to me:

„I can see you have been fighting. Do you want to tell me about it?" (Listen without judging and without wanting to find out who is 'right'.)
„Yes, this is really awkward. Can you find a solution together or do you need my help?" (wait)
„Mmm, yes. I can see, this is not so easy." (wait)

Use connecting instead of separating words:
'you two', 'together'.

„How can you solve this? Do you have any ideas? There is no hurry, we have time."

Illness

Drop frightening sentences that make things worse:
„For god`s sake, what happened! This looks terrible!"
('Catastrophic announcements'). Neither make it seem insignificant. The child does not feel it is taken seriously if it hears: „It is not so bad, you know!"
Of course it is very bad for the child!
What the child needs is empathy and approval (confirmation, validation).
But please no pitying: „Poor thing, you!" - Pity makes them weak.

This helps:
„I am with you."
„I am here."
In the case of an emergency just use this one sentence again and again. Be there, hold its hand. When my daughter was twelve years old she had a bicycle accident and was lying in an induced coma for one week. Every day I sat with her, talked to her, and silently massaged her feet.
I was sure that she felt my presence.

Calming, asserting, strengthening:
„Every human being can become ill."
„Yes, now this needs a little bit of patience."
„Yes, this hurts."
„Yes, this is awful (awkward, unpleasant). I will stay with you, we will get through this together."
„The doctors will help you. The medicine tastes somewhat funny, I know, but it will help. You can add some juice to make it taste better."

„It's great how you are coping with this! You are just the perfect patient. You will see, in a few days things will be better." (Patients need to be 'patient'!)

Before you take your child to a hospital it is wise to prepare them on an intellectual and factual level. Go and have a look, make a visit if possible.
After a hospital experience it is good to do a little 'trauma-processing-work', or simpler said, digest it: talk about it, draw, paint, possibly work with clay – as long as the child needs it and shows an interest. Offer the material, make it available but don`t push it.

Just be there: It is a wonderful experience
getting down on eye-level and spend some precious time with a kid.

Lying

There exist many and different reasons for lying:
- fear of humiliation or punishment.

In a friendly kind way: *"Do you know the reason you did not tell the truth? What are you afraid of? What do you think will happen?"*

- Taking revenge (when the child feels they are being treated unfairly or are being hurt).

"I can imagine that you feel terribly hurt, when you do something like that. To insult someone is very serious and not okay. What would help you? What do you need to repair this and feel better yourself again?"

- A lot of imagination (telling stories and mixing up the truth). Younger children can have difficulties distinguishing between fairy tales and the truth.

"Aha, this sounds very interesting. A magnificent story! And how is it in real life?"
"This is a wonderful story. You have a lot of imagination. Would you like to write it down?"

- Wanting to get attention (boasting).

"Aha, very interesting. Now, kids, did you hear what Noah has to tell us? Yes, you are very strong. Could you push the tables with the others? That would be a great help!"
Possibly start utilising and diverting this feeling of power immediately and strengthen his self-esteem.

- Wanting to belong
- Compensating a sense of inferiority

Do not expose the child but accept its feelings, wishes and desires (longing). Talk about them.

**When parenting becomes understanding,
clear and free from punishment,
the child does not need to be afraid or be ashamed.**

Coco and Khaleesi having fun drumming on a chair

Media
(TV, Mobiles, Computer)

The German neuroscientist Manfred Spitzer has written a whole book about it: „Digitale Demenz". There are many opinions about this subject - I share his.

I know that this is a hotly debated, controversial and complex issue. Exactly because of this I want to make my comments brief here. Otherwise it could go on for ever!

The most important thing is to state age appropriate exposure:

No movies for babies or toddlers.

Kindergarten-age children moderate exposure. Choose the films together, talk about the content and discuss afterwards.

DVDs are more practical because there is the possibility of repetition: the children can digest better.

Important: the movie must be watched to the end otherwise there can be too much tension.

Discuss beforehand:
"What`s in the program?"
"How long does it last?"
"What`s the content, the theme?"
We can ask older kids:
"What do you think? Is this movie appropriate for your age?"

Mobiles, Computers and the Internet:
Real life contacts, meetings, playing / experiencing together are all important for social development and competence . Only when we meet humans can we learn to be together and cope with each other.
Teenagers often get very lonely when they spend too much time in front of the television or are busy with their smart phones.
Have clear rules, mobile-free-zones (means *without* mobile!):
"All our meals and the family-meetings are mobile-free. Also when we go for a bike ride or a hike or similar events outdoors."
They can use the mobile for arranging dates / activities with friends.
Watch your own consumption and minimise it for the sake of the children. Inform them about the dangers with the internet without frightening them. Inform yourself. Embed the idea of security and safety. Build a stable trust-relation so that the children take it upon themselves to tell you about things. Respect their privacy.
Use the media creatively: for research, learning, quench the thirst for knowledge.
If necessary, buy intelligent learning-games and join in the play ... if permitted!

Sweets, Candy and Chewing-Gum

One mother reports:
Sweets are always around within reach but the three year-old should always ask first if they can have some. The mother will say yes or no! (For the child this is torture!)
I ask: „What for?"
"So he will learn, this is training!"
„Then you should go to the circus right away with him!" I say spontaneously. She then realises that it is similar to animal training.

„This would be the same as if I put tea and sweets on the table in front of your nose but you would have to ask first if you were allowed to take some. How would this make you feel?"

Observation in a shop:
On the counter there is a small plate of free sweets. A child wants to take some, the mother says in a kind way: „Darling, you know that we have a deal, don`t you." The girl looks at the sales-lady, looks at the mother and again at the sweets – and then they pass by without another word. The secret of this deal will never be unveiled but it must have been a good one!

Another mother complains that her children always take the sweets without asking. "Where do you keep them?" "O well, I cannot lock everything away!" „Why not? And why are they there anyway? Who is buying them?"

Whining children are not easy to bear for any of us. Limit sweets and keep to the limits firmly and in a friendly way.
Be like a rock in the breakers!

"I am sorry, dear, today you have already had your chewing-gum. Tomorrow you can have one piece again." (Telling exactly helps.)
"This afternoon we will each have two pieces of chocolate, I am already looking forward to it!"

"In the holidays you can have an ice-cream every day. Then we will play I scream – you scream – we all scream: ice creeeeaaammm uuuuaaaahhhh!"
"Too much sugar is not good but we can enjoy a little!"

When it is important for you, you can define a certain time (on the clock) when it will be.
Note: NOT for dessert!
And also not as a means of pressure to make the children eat up, this is most harmful!
Or you could introduce the monthly sweet-box for older children. At the beginning of the month it is filled (define with what and how much. Sweets that the children are given from others also go into the box). When it is empty, it is empty. So the children learn how to ration themselves and wait till the next month.
Watch your own behaviour concerning the 'sweet tooth'. Sweets are 'emotional food', that does not really feed or satisfy us! On top of that the brain does not have a barrier concerning sugar. So we have to stop ourselves and protect the children from sugar-addiction.

Rather allow more often being close, kind wrestling (tussle, scuffle)
– this is 'sweets for the heart'
and replaces sweets and the pacifier!

Loreena is so proud! She had just learned to ride the bicycle.

Pacifier / Dummy, Crying and Comforting

A mother wants to get rid of the pacifier / dummy but she still keeps it, not setting any limits.
„I hold her in my arms and give her the dummy. When I give it to her she stops crying very quickly." (That is the point!) „How long can you bear the crying of your daughter?" „Well, I *do* bear it …" – Really?
Should we donate the dummy to the Easter-bunny or to Santa Claus? For the animals in the forest? For other children? My advice is not to do so. It is an absurd lie! The mother, the father are the best comforters. No replacing the last lost dummy.

„Now you are big (old) enough. I will hold you. You want me to sing? To caress you? Where?"

Bear it! Let them cry till it is really over. Most of the time it is our own pain that arises, and we are not so fond of bearing it. Maybe as children we were not allowed to cry until the feeling was exhausted. Children give us so many opportunities to experience much, to explore our own feelings and to change habits.
We have a song in the German speaking countries that goes somewhat like this: "Heal heal bliss, three days rain, three days snow, then it does not hurt anymore!" This implicates that it 'should be over' too soon!
I recommend not to use it because the child should be allowed to cry it all out as long as it needs it.
Tears wash stress-hormones out of the body!

„I am glad that you can show your feelings so well! We will wait here till you have finished. Take time."
(This relaxes.)

A friend told us that a boy got a tractor from the dummy-fairy after giving his dummy away. „Yes, indeed a good idea …. and when I stop smoking at 16 I'll get a scooter, and when I am 18, a car … etc." Who is inventing this rubbish? Are we not conscious of the consequences?

The reward is the *pride, to have succeeded*, to be so big already!

When Amelie is crying at night, her mother comes and gets into the spoon-position with her which gives her safety and warmth. It also helped when she said:
"Let it all come out."

A father complains that his four year old daughter wants to have her dummy again although she did not need it any more. „Where did she get it?", I ask. "Oh, it was lying in my car!"

It would be better to really be brave and let the dummies disappear so as to make the children proud:

„Children that can ride a bicycle don`t need a dummy anymore! This is so revolting (ghastly)!"
Exaggerate with humour, awake the joy and pride in the child.

Sometimes it helps when another child takes notice (similarly with nappies) and remarks:

„What? You still have a dummy? (need nappies?)"
An adult who has a good relationship with the child can also do this, when it is said in a kind but astonished way without sounding like a trick.

When the child takes the dummy from a younger sibling:

"I see, you want to be a baby again? Come here, I 'll cradle you! It was so lovely when you were a baby, we can play this as often as you like. The dummy is for the baby and it stays in its bed."

In Bern (Switzerland) I found a dummy-tree in the Museum of Conversation where children can hang their dummies with colourful ribbons. What a grand idea!
This could be the procedure:

1. First talk it over with the child:
"You are big now, and already going to play-group, ... can ride a bicycle / ... can dress alone. This is fantastic! Now we will choose a day on the calendar when we will go to the dummy-tree and decorate it with all your dummies and nice glittery ribbons. We will have a nice celebration."

2. Choose the tree or bush together, make a connection with it, play there often, talk about it.

3. Cross off every day on the calendar together and repeatedly tell him/ her how proud you are of them.

4. Plan the celebration with the child, ask what she/ he wants to do, play, eat and drink. This togetherness is the most important thing of it all.

5. Go there on this special day, with the dummies on ribbons. Present them to the tree and hang them high enough, but visible so that „everybody can see, that you are dummy-free now."

„To be dummy-free enables you to sing and talk much clearer!"

6. Bear it, don`t go soft if sadness or anger is arising. Comfort the child and take them in your arms, see it through:
„Yes, I know this is not easy. You will see, you will do it. Together we will do it!"

And sing the dummy-good-bye-song if you like:

Dummy-good-bye
Dummy-good-bye, if it hurts you can cry,
Have been good friends for so long,
Now it is time you are gone,
Dummy-good-bye, if it hurts you can cry.

Dummy wow wow, you can go now,
We hang you in this tree
I am now dummy-free,
Dummy wow wow, you can go now.

Dummy oh oh, now you can go,
Loved you so much before,
Don`t need you any more,
Dummy oh oh, now you can go.

Dummy old boy, I sing with joy,
Can better sing and talk,
Don`t need you for a walk,
Dummy old boy, I sing with joy.

With the same Melody
brrr, brrr, brrr, brrr or other sounds with the tongue

and trallallalla…..

I am big - wow, I let you go NOW!

Bye, dummies, bye!

Rules

(Through 'Family-Council' ... 63, or 'Class-Council' ...
160 to the rules. Also see 'Quarrelling' ... 153

The most important shortly here:
1. Put the rules up *together*
(Then the 'we' is justified!)
And: when the children have helped set the rules and agreed that they are also important for themselves, they will find them easier to follow.
2. Express the rules positively and in present tense (state clearly how you want them done).
3. Just a few and make them clear.
4. Phrase them comprehensible.
5. Have friendly consequences for example when rules are not followed:
„So sorry, now I don`t like to cut you an apple."

Example rules:
1. We are friendly to each other.
2. We listen to each other.
3. We help each other.
4. We do our jobs.
5. We arrive on time.
6. We tidy up.
7. We can run around outside.

(Avoid 'we shall' or 'we will' because this means it will happen in the future but we want it now!)
Important:
When you request or express a *wish* this leaves the options open, we give the child a choice!
„I would like you to ... Can you pass me ...? Thank you."
But *rules* are followed by all. **Only by living together in this way a family can function effectively.**

Dry and Clean: Nappies, Potty, WC, Washing ys.
(also see 'Bed-Wetting' ... 77)

Getting dry

Most children are dry by four years old. It is best not to make a big fuss about it and to cope with this issue in 'a matter-of-fact' way, as far as possible. The child will mature into it.

It is easier to practise this 'getting dry' in the summer months, outdoors.

When the child is urinating outside it does not matter.

„The meadow drinks your pee, and the grass will grow very well!"

„You can water the bush (the tree) here, they will like it. We can add a little water now."

„Don`t worry, this happens. Luckily I have brought a second pair of trousers with us."

If you always take clothes with you it will ease the situation. In case this is embarrassing, just think of the numerous city-dogs and where they all urinate!

This way you have an answer ready and a solution in case your child urinates somewhere in public. I think children`s urine is almost like water, not bad at all! It is warm, panties dry fast, no big deal. You can finish with panties by just not buying a new bag and showing the child: now it is finished. You are grown.

When you notice the signs at home that your child gives, you can get the potty and put them on it. Wait with them until what comes, comes. If it takes time tell a story and admire the 'present' afterwards:

„Super! Now the pee is in the potty and now we can pour it into the toilet and it goes on a big journey to the ocean! Bye!"

Also admire the 'big business'. Be in awe for what came out of such a small body! The child is very proud that it can produce for us such a present with his / her own body.

"Great, this is going well! Soon you won't need nappies anymore! You are so grown up already!"

If the child smears their faeces / 'poo', don't scold them.

"Ah, so you wanted to try that out. Now, let's clean you up and then together we can clean up everything else."

Say in a positive way what you want:

"We leave the poo in the potty, I will give you play-dough to kneed and play with afterwards."

When you go to the toilet leave the door open, put the potty beside you and let the child watch. They want to copy us anyway.

There are smaller seats you can buy to put on top of the toilet seat and little stools for children to make it easier for them to climb up and sit.

Calming sentences, adapted to age:

"I am sure, in time you will do it. There is no hurry."
"Come now, let's clean this up together."
"I will show you how you can rinse your trousers yourself, no problem."

Simon has urinated beside the potty. He also empties what was in it and does not clean it up. His mother is upset as she wants him to do it properly.

Exercise relaxation:

"No problem, this can happen."
"Come on I show you how this is done, we can clean it up together."

Loreena and Nepomuk are enjoying
their flower-pot-bath in the garden

Washing

All children love water because it is our natural original element. We were in the womb in the 'fertile water' for nine months before birth. Actually, we love to go 'back home' to water.

We can awaken the joy for water again by letting children play with water. Together in the bath-tub, in the sand-pit, with the hose, with the watering-can, by emptying, filling and refilling cups and jugs.

Turning washing and showering into a game. When soap and shampoo irritate use less or leave them out altogether. – The child gets clean without it!

One boy used to play in a well in the forest for hours but at home he would have a huge tantrum when it was time for his bath. Here it helped when the parents allowed him to play in the bath-tub and get clean at the same time!

In the kindergarten the following happened:
two girls got hold of the liquid-soap-dispenser and had their hands full of soap-bubbles. Another time they washed their hair and came out of the toilet with totally wet hair and clothes.
Possible positive reaction:

"Ah, so today you two want to be really clean! So much foam and loads of bubbles! You like that, hmm? Yes, I totally understand. It smells so good!"
So if I want to save soap I can always put the dispenser away so that the children cannot use it themselves.
"Oh, I see, today you even washed your hair yourselves! Your mothers will be so proud of you. You are so grown up. So, let's give you some towels now. Do you want to dry yourself or do you need my help?"

One pre-school-teacher commented: „But if I am so accommodating they will want to do it more often!"

Yes, we think that would be the logical outcome. Yet, children function *psycho*logically. When the situation gets little attention it will become boring quite quickly. They know: there is nothing to be gained (not even punishment or scolding).

**When we see the positive in any situation
and emphasise it,
the atmosphere becomes more relaxed
and we have a more healthy and loving
relationship
with the children.**

Being quiet

Four adults and two children (9 and 10 years old) go for a walk. The 9-year-old Elena walks ahead with the two men. 10-year-old Claus is walking between the two women, holding their hands and talking without interruption, telling stories and jokes. The two women would like to talk to each other.

"Claus, it is really interesting what you have been telling us. I love to listen to you. Now I would like to tell your mother something. What do you think, will you be able to let us talk for five minutes? Look, here is my watch."
Claus is not willing to try. I stay firm and friendly.

"I am sure you will be able to do this. Let's see how long you can do it for."
Firmly (reassuringly) I still hold his hand. I start talking to his mother; he is interrupting, and starts to sing in gibberish, loudly. I smile at him, shake my head:
"It has only been one minute and I would like to finish what I was saying. Then it's your turn."

We two women talk for about ten minutes and Claus is completely quiet, calmly walking between us, absorbed in his own thoughts, still holding our hands. As the conversation comes to an end I ask him:

"Claus, how are you now?"
"Fine!" he says smiling and seems very content (satisfied).

I give him my appreciation:
„It was great, how that worked!"

Making a call:
„I would like to talk to Elisa for 10 minutes. What could you do whilst I talk?"
„Would you like to say Hello at the beginning?"

A doctor lets his three-year-old daughter say hello to all callers, also patients, then she is quiet and carries on playing. It has become just like a ritual: she feels taken seriously and is then quite happy. Also those that are calling enjoy it and are often surprised to hear this friendly child`s voice!

If my telephone-call is disturbed repeatedly it is followed by a **'friendly' consequence** which does not mean that I have to smile always! It means I am talking in a neutral, **not angry** way. The child is not allowed to visit his / her playmate:

„I am so sorry. I like to talk to my friend without being disturbed. When I can do this, then you can go to visit your friend. I am sure this is possible"

Sleeping

The most used and most harmful sentence is:
„You have to go to sleep now!"
It is paradox: sleeping means relaxing. This cannot be forced!
One of my two sons had difficulties falling asleep when he was fourteen. Then he told me about something he had discovered:
„Mum, I have found the answer. In a movie I saw, soldiers had to stay awake. They told themselves over and over: I have to fall asleep right now! I have to fall asleep right now! So I thought, what if I turned this around and so I said to myself: 'I have to stay awake at all costs!' ' I must hear the next tolling of the bell!' Lo and behold – pow! – I fell asleep immediately! It worked!"

What is useful:

„You don`t have to sleep. You can just lie in your bed and read for a while ..."
The older sibling is allowed to have the lights on for ten minutes longer.
„You can whisper to your teddy-bear a good-night-story so he can fall asleep easier."
„We, the parents, have a free evening now (time for ourselves), (mummy-daddy-time) and want to be alone. Tomorrow we will play with you again."

Even better: 'roll out the day' - relive the day before switching off the lights. Talk about all the beautiful experiences you had and enjoy them again.

Mention the definite plans for the next day and that you are looking forward to them.

When the child gets out of bed put it into bed again quietly, calmly and firmly, making no big deal of it. Whosoever gets angry has lost the game. It helps letting a partner take over so you can do something else.

The calmer you react the more effective it is. Talk during the day with the child about what could help him / her to stay in bed.

A very successful idea is to introduce a 'mummy's evening and 'daddy`s evening'. Write on the calendar in different colours who is in turn and show it to the child. Stick to it, no matter how much the child does not want it.

Often children experience a whole 'circus' when daddy comes home in the evening. Fathers enjoy this very much too and then suddenly it is time to stop - the children should calm down quickly. Do you recognise this?

It does not work. Take time to play wildly if there is enough time to calm down or make the wild time shorter.

The evening should become more and more quiet and boring. It helps to plan in enough time. If you stress, the children get more anxious, more impatient and more demanding.

It can be to your advantage to introduce the clock. It is a friendly, neutral authority.

„At eight thirty it is mum and dad`s leisure time. We still have time for a story. If we brush our teeth right now we can have even more time. What do you prefer to do first: brush your teeth or put on your pyjamas?"
(Possibility of choice diminishes a power struggle.)

Toddlers can be carried around:
"Now we say good-night to the lamp. Look the curtains are very tired, and the table is falling asleep, and the chairs ... etc."

Naming everything, talking slower and quieter can produce miracles.
(I almost fall asleep myself, it is so calming!)
When I let go, I radiate this mood to the child and he or she can also let go.

Allow yourself the luxury to let the child fall asleep by itself at any time and see how relaxing this can be ...
Maybe during the holidays? Like Medea in the dog-basket – and the dog has positioned himself beside her!

Sexuality

An extract from my book „Die integrative Erziehung im Vorschulalter" („The integrative education in pre-school-age", German only):

Scene in a crèche: Today three girls and two boys are building a cosy cave to crawl into with the help of a young apprentice. When the apprentice leaves, the children are playing calmly and peacefully so I let them play on their own. I am in the other room with the other children but with one ear to what they are doing. Three-year old Sarina comes to me and says:
„Now nobody is allowed to enter our room!" The group-leader responsible finds this suspicious but I tell him to let them as I think it's very nice, how they are 'discovering each other'.
And how they discovered each other!!
After a while I go and knock at their door, I am allowed in. Dense mist! Mattresses, floor - everything covered in baby-powder, cream and discarded nappies.
All the children, without their panties, are deeply absorbed in changing each others' nappies. One is tapping powder out of a giant can – puff – puff - :
„So it will smell beautiful in here," Mira informs me smiling, "and if I could just get her nappy on!" Normally she does not wear one. Micki is also beaming at me and explodes with his news: „Girls have two bums!"
„Yes they have a vagina!" I say, to name the sex organ by its proper name. But he sticks to his two 'bums' and is proud and surprised at the same time with what he has found out.
The children wash themselves and help to tidy up. Corinna`s mother is happy with this:

„Oh, she loves to play this at home! It's great that they were allowed to play this here, as well!"

I am smiling to myself; and as the person in charge sees the 'nice mess' he also nods grinning. I am glad that the children could have such a pleasant experience! What does it matter if the mattresses do have a little cream on them, everything smells so good from the baby-powder – the floor can easily be cleaned! The children are happy and have experienced a sensual, interesting afternoon and so they are content. The children have had a lesson in sexual education without realising. Sexual instruction starts when it is needed which means when it is asked for.

Children love to play 'doctor', so we should let them explore their bodies undisturbed. Often our own experiences come to the surface: it is good to remember. Were we allowed to? Were we disturbed? Scolded? Shamed? How did it feel? What are we afraid of (now)?

Naming the vagina and penis by their correct names is best from the earliest age when changing nappies. Name or sing about all the body-parts when bathing the baby so the child feels good about his / her whole body.

When children examine each other:

„You are careful with each other, aren`t you?"
„When something hurts you say STOP. And the other child has to stop." „It is important to me that you feel comfortable."

The last sentence can just be thought by yourself. This also has an effect.

Our own attitude to sexuality, to our own body is transmitted to the child. It is advantageous if the child believes that the body is precious, beautiful and something to take care of.

Protection from sexual abuse
The child must be allowed to say 'NO'! Do not demand their kisses, hugs, the shaking of hands or other similar body-contacts if the child does not want it.
The child's intimate space must be respected. From a responsible age he/she must be permitted to lock him/herself in their room, bath or toilet. We knock the door and enter only after given permission.
„*When it feels weird you say 'stop' or 'no' and go away." No one is permitted to touch you where you don`t want it."*
Someone recalled: „My father often tickled me so much that I wet my pants. I was already going to preschool and was really ashamed. However, because of that I could not tell him to stop. I did not want him to think me a kill joy!" This is how much children love their parents!

Teenagers
I gave several sex-education-books to my own children when they were teenagers. I brought them from the library, and asked them to look at them and tell me which ones would be the most appropriate ones for their age. This was so we could talk in a more relaxed way about this subject and I soon realised that they knew much more than I presumed. This set me at ease.
When they are dating a boy - or girl and going out it is enough to ask just the once:

„Prevention – all clear?"
„Do you need anything?"
„I wish you fun!"
„You can always come to me. I am here."

No warnings (embarrassing!), no reminding them of the agreed time to come back (getting on one`s nerves!) and no asking questions (useless!). They should be allowed to come back by themselves and tell you what they want to.

> **When we truly, really listen to them**
> **without criticising or advising**
> **they are able to come to us**
> **in confidence.**

When my three kids went to school, they had cooking and baking-lessons. The teacher said, they were not allowed to form the sexual organs when making manikins. (In Switzerland they are called 'Grittibänz'). Of-course I let them do it at home, they had great fun!

Stealing

In the human brain there is no 'drawer' for 'possessions'. In the early childhood everything belongs to everybody because the child cannot differentiate. With a great deal of struggle she / he learns what 'mine' or 'yours' means. In the beginning it cannot do any differently. Later on the child may not want to because it has been spoilt or because it cannot wait or does not want to keep the rules of the society (family or group).
The child may also steal because it feels it is not getting enough, being deprived of something (things, care, love), or because it feels lonely, sad, or as if it did not belong: it wants to compensate by taking things belonging to others.
The child can become a thief to take revenge, to feel better, greater or more powerful. The child compensates its feeling of unworthiness by stealing.

One mother told me of a boy who, when playing with her children at their home always took something precious away with him. I suggested that she prepared a box containing nice things that she knew he might like and to show it to him right at the beginning of his visit with the offer that he can choose one thing as a present.

„What is it that you would like to take home with you today?"

She had the feeling that it might also be a souvenir to remind him of the nice play-time he had had with her children because his home was not so pleasant.

The stealing ceased immediately: he did not need to any more.
In the play-group or in the parent/child singing classes I always lend my toys, small instruments or play-animals when the children ask me for them. The children are very proud, pleased and always bring them back.

If something is missing never ask:
„Who has pinched it?"
This sentence is counterproductive and of no use!
In the family or class we can for example act like this:

„Unfortunately my wallet has disappeared. Maybe I mislaid it. Has anybody seen it? I would be grateful if you all could help me search for it!"
„Now we shall all leave the room and each one of us can go into the classroom alone."

In this way the thief gets the chance to put the stolen object back without being forced to reveal him/herself. We do not even have to express a feeling of disappointment /sadness and certainly we utter no judgement (because this would be moralizing which is completely unnecessary) as this would mean shaming them which makes everything worse. They are ashamed anyway because they *know* they did something not quite 'correct'.

*„Unfortunately the CD has not appeared up to now. I imagine somebody wanted to take it home because they are so fond of the music. When it has been given back I can copy it for all who want it. It would be best to put it in my drawer when nobody is here. I don`t have to know who **borrowed** it ..."*

When young children have taken something I often say:

"Aha, the car has gone on a holiday to your home! Lovely that it has come back again! Did you have fun together?"

To all kids:

"You can simply ask me, I love to lend my stuff to you!"

Help the child, don`t leave it alone or shame it:

"I can help you and come with you. We can take that back together."

"Unfortunately it is already broken. I am sure you will replace it. You can buy a new one with your pocket-money and so make it up."

In a kindergarten two girls opened bags belonging to the other children and took out fruit which they then ate.
Now it was important to approach them in a kind way because their conduct could have been for any number of reasons:
It might be that they felt they lacked something or that they had food in their own bags they were not interested in. Other people's food is always more interesting!
I always presume that there is no bad intention behind it. So how can we react?
It is good to get down at eye-level and stay friendly. Only like this can the children open up to me and I can find out more about the circumstances:

"Oh, I see, you have unpacked fruit from the other children's bags and tried them. How did they taste? I was just thinking: what do you think they will eat then?"

Try to listen to the tone of your voice: is there still a bit of a reproach in it? Are you capable of dropping that?
"How do you think will they feel?"
*"**Luckily** there is still something left."*
"So come on, let`s take your bags and see what you two have got. Aha, there is some bread ... etc. You don`t like that much?"
"Now we can divide all this up to share. What do you think? Could you help me cut? Here is a knife. Which one wants to cut first?"

We could ask their parents if it is possible to give them fruit. But no 'telling tales' to the parents as this affects their trust in us. Whatever happens in the group we must solve it ourselves. The parents must be able to trust that the teachers solve the problems by themselves and that the child is well taken care of.

I recommend the introduction of a **'sharing-plate'** in all play-groups and kindergartens. Everything is offered on the plate and cut and arranged by the children so they can share and everyone can try the things they would like. The teachers are models and also put their fruit on the sharing plate.

Disturbing

School-age

Children who make troubles want to tell us that they *have* troubles. It is their SOS. If we can respond appropriately the children will cease their disruptive behaviour: they won't need it any more.

Rudolf Dreikurs teaches us to ignore / not give attention to the non-desired behaviours and to give attention without mentioning (neither positive nor negative) behaviour when the child shows the desired behaviour.

Looking at everything now I can see that I have had positive experiences whenever I have asked the 'fire-raiser' to be the 'fire-fighter'.

Example:

Mirko always switches off the light in the corridor because then the girls scream so 'wonderfully' shrill – a well-established game for all involved!

Scolding and reminding results in the opposite of what is wanted: he loves it even more because he has a fleeting sensation of success when he annoys me too! I give him the sought after attention by naming him the protector of the light- switch, my 'light-guardian'. He is grinning and takes on the job: from that moment the corridor stays lit. At first this was very much a surprise to me, then a joy! Of-course this was mentioned later (not immediately) in the class-meeting:

„I am pleased at how well this is working, we always have light in the corridor now!"

After two weeks or so someone else can take over and do this job, and Mirko can do something else that is important. (That makes him *feel* important.)

Marco and the Stop-Watch
1st Grade

Marco is continually disturbing the lesson and today he has no eyes or ears for the class-activities, only for his stop-watch.

How can I win him over in my music-lesson? I admire the watch respectfully and integrate it spontaneously into the class:

"This is great, you know! Now you can time how long it takes for all of you to sit in a circle!"

Very quickly all the children sit and he proudly tells us how long it took. This we do repeatedly after every moving sequence. I let the children move to music. Marco times how long it takes.

I say: *„Oh yes, I always wanted to know how long this piece of music lasted!"*

And as we repeat the tasks he times them again. He seems very content.

Then one of the children gets hurt in a collision between two of them and so we sit down together to talk about it. Marco starts belching noisily. I manage to totally ignore him, give my attention to the others and do not react either to Marco or to the other children's comments.

Finally, the children stop reacting to Marco. Marco makes a last, long, loud belch and then lets himself fall backwards out of the circle. As he gets up he draws closer to me so I address him and include him in the ongoing conversation. He does not belch any more.

At the end of the lesson I distribute star-stickers to all the children to be stuck on the class-list because all of them had worked well. Marco asks surprised: „I also may stick one to the list?"

"Yes for sure! You have been cooperating very well. You calculated the time with your watch and told us how long it took!"

"But I was belching!"

"Yes, I know. You probably wanted to know what I would do, how I would react, right?"

He grins and shrugs his shoulders.

"You wanted to provoke me?"

He nods. Still smiling we say good bye to each other.

Ignoring the negative conduct and giving him attention as soon as this behaviour stopped, without referring to it, worked. Funny: in the end Marco mentioned it himself. He really wanted to know what would happen. So, it was not necessary to belch any more.

Later I thought he might have behaved like this in the circle because he was embarrassed and insecure about what would happen after the crash of the two children. Maybe he expected scolding and he felt uncomfortable.

Reminder: the children do not collect stickers for themselves but contribute to the class-list. When it is full we celebrate with dancing to their own music or having a snack together. (Nothing expensive but fun!)

It is important that children with difficulties can put stickers on the list for every small positive act so they will get a higher self-esteem and would not need to disturb so much anymore. They love to contribute to the community.

With 'jobs' (responsibilities) it works out much better!

Finally I introduced the 'jobs' in a music-class. I found it very hard to get the children to join in the lesson. While the boys were running around making mischief, the girls were just sitting around and they always seemed to be bored no matter what I offered.

I had the impression that I was always trying to get one group going whilst having to stop the others! What a painful and hopeless situation! Of-course I had tried several integrative ideas from the training, like the collecting of stars for good behaviour or the `mini-class-meeting`. I had tried Mària Kenessey`s `feeling-training` using the emotions-barometer (every one telling or showing with pictures how they felt) and my own integrative songs. I also changed my teaching methods several times. These steps brought some relief and small improvements but they did not work as well as I would have liked. I wanted to motivate these children even more to join in or work productively by themselves. So then I introduced the 'jobs'. One boy from Turkey called Mehmed, preferred most of all to ring a bell, strike the gong or hit the cymbals and was very reluctant to join in the circle: so I nominated him to be our first 'bell-master'. His job was now to ring the bell to tell the children when they should gather together in a circle.

Here he is standing now forming the circle for me! He is ringing the bell very seriously and proudly and is calling all the children together while I sit patiently on my chair and watch silently! (How soothing for my strained voice and nerves!) He is supported by the second bell-master with whom he is taking turns and who reminds him in case he forgets his job. Two other children are 'stop-watch-masters'. They measure the time on the stop-watch - how long it takes all the children to sit in a circle, or how long it takes until all are ready or how long we have for an exercise, a song etc. Two more are responsible for the wardrobe, and two for the cupboard to help with tidying up the instruments. Two take control in the middle and at the end of the lesson: it is their responsibility to see that everything is in its proper place, nothing forgotten or left behind.

After the holidays there will be a change. Oh my Goodness, how different this lesson is with the jobs, it was running smoothly! Like water! Well, it still took quite a while until they all came into the circle, till everything was clean and they were still – but it was not for me to worry anymore! Now I had these responsible chiefs and they did their jobs really well. The children had much more motivation than before, proud and full of enthusiasm with everything they did. They helped each other more than before. Yes they almost created competition between themselves to carry chairs, drums and to help with putting everything in the cupboard. After this lesson I decided to introduce 'the jobs idea' into all of my other groups and classes – I did, and I am glad I did!

From my book „Die integrative Pädagogik in der Musikalischen Grundschule" (in German only).

When children challenge us it is a present for us. Newly formed brain-cells only stay alive if they are challenged regularly and radically!

Quarrelling (Between Siblings), Class-Council and Rules

Quarrels – part of (siblings`) life
and siblings` love!

... and reconciliation is happening - over and over again!

„Siblings love each other to quarrel" is the title of a book which I bought and read as my three children were still small. I was desperate: there was always two of them together against the third. I was always taken in by their screaming and ran to them to soothe or settle (which made things worse, of-course)! At that time I did not know about Mària Kenessey. The book calmed me down, it said that siblings` quarrels are something absolutely normal. Every healthy human being has his / her own opinion which may differ from each other. Or both want the same.

We adults can practise being role-models. We can ask ourselves the following questions:

How do we deal with different opinions between adults?

What is our „quarrelling-culture" that we bring from our parents' home?

How do we (did we) solve problems?

What do we do when angry?

Can we show grief?

There exists several reasons for quarrelling:

1. Wanting to get attention
2. Wanting to express discontent, anger, a grudge or frustration
3. Letting out steam (suppressed body-power)
4. Practising being able to achieve something.
5. Wanting to be right (to win)
etc.

Constructive coping with conflict:

1. Wait. (Is it really dangerous?)
2. Interfere when there is danger:

„Stop! This hurts! I do not want you to hurt each other."

3. Talking in the „you-two, both"- language, using connecting words:

„Is there a disagreement between you two?"

4. Listen. Give no solutions:

„Oh yes, this is really unpleasant!"

5. Don`t divide into victim and victimiser!
You will never really find out who started the argument and by the way, it doesn't help anyone at all.
Wait and listen. Build in self-responsibility:
„What do you think? Can you find a solution by yourselves or do you need help?"
"What is your proposal? Do you have any ideas on how you two could solve this?"

Asking them questions develops their sense of self-responsibility and boosts their competence for solving conflicts.
Mostly children offer amazing suggestions!

If they are quarrelling over an object and cannot find an appropriate solution the thing "goes on a holiday". Language for young kids:

"This stick goes on a holiday till tomorrow. Then you can practise playing safely with it again."
"This is hurtful for the doll. She will now rest for a while. You can play with it again later."

Actually it is not really about the object but always about emotions like envy, jealousy, the sensation of not getting enough or being treated unfairly.

Older children like it when I talk like this to them, they feel taken seriously and grown-up. I give trust-in-advance:
"I'll look after this now until you can come up with a good solution."

One mother with integrative knowledge wrote to me:
"What mostly gets me down at the moment is the non-stop-**quarrels** between my two "sweeties" (Eve, 5 and David, 3)
Sometimes I try to ignore it but they won`t stop at all and end up hitting each other! When I do a puzzle with both of them they almost tear it to shreds. At mealtimes, everywhere, anywhere scenes and noise all the time! They raise hell – I am finished!

Every morning I intend not to shout at them but I just cannot bear it! Today there wasn't even a five minute break between quarrelling. We went outside but there it was the same: each one wanted the same helmet for the bicycle, each the same swing, each to go down a different street of-course …….

I think ahead of the dreadful weekends which I actually find such a shame.

And then of-course the fears: if I cannot cope with the elder one now, what will it be like when they are both older? How will this all turn out???

Eve provokes her brother David until he finally screams - and when I try to say something „neutral" she just grins, then I really explode.

I was so fed up and worn out that I ran away – but then Eve bit David ………

Peaceful greetings from two sleeping mice and a deranged and physically exhausted mother who still has sooooo much to learn!!!!!

Continued:

After reflecting on the evening before yesterday I realised that I cannot continue like this and that I am at the end of my tether I decided to be like the famous „rock in the breakers" , to keep calm and firm ….

And it **worked perfectly**! Yesterday was a wonderful day with the children. I did not try to manage a hundred of my own things simultaneously but committed myself completely to the children!

And then I was even rewarded with some leisure-time as a present on top! Several times they went out into the garden together all alone and played cooking like world-champions and there were no huge quarrels – isn`t that super??!!"

Yes, that is fantastic! This mother remembered and found the solution by herself. She realised that it was about this hundred percent attention (not the whole time, this is impossible and also not desirable!) When the children are satisfied they are contented and play peacefully together again.

Peacefully united and sunk into play

One mother reports in the parenting-training that she had great success with her children by letting each of them uninterruptedly and freely talk for 5 minutes (using a watch or sand-watch), during which they could express everything unlimited (also showing their anger).

From my book „Die integrative Pädagogik in der Musikalischen Grundschule" (The integrative Pedagogy in the Primary Music school, German only):

School-age
Conflict and reconciliation

When I studied the integrative method we concentrated on the issues of dealing with violence, conflicts and reconciliation. When we say 'excuse me' we are hoping that others will take away our feelings of guilt. 'Do not accuse me – but ex-cuse me.' (The German 'Ent-schuldigung' would mean 'de-guilt me' in direct translation). However, with an honest „I am so sorry!" we are showing real remorse and a willingness to make things better which creates a better feeling at both sides. Remorse, together with deep understanding and discernment naturally produces improvement and positive change. We should also ask about the others' feelings using the 'you two-form':

„Are you two sad?" or
„Are you two angry?" *„Do you have a problem with each other?" „Do you have a conflict together?"*
Give them 'take up' time and then ask:
„What do you need?"
„What do you both need?"
I took all these useful scripts to heart and tried them out in the Forest-Kindergarten and in the Music School where I had some wonderful experiences. I made up a song that was loved by the children because it helped them to cope with their difficulties and conflicts, to be able to say sorry in a good natured way and to make friends again. The children often asked for this song

when quarrelling, when they needed comforting or help in making the peace. Sometimes it was just for fun after an argument that ended peacefully. It is the „I am sorry-song".

A reminder:
There are no 'bad ones', only 'hurt ones'.

Class-rules by a Class-Council

This is explained as follows by *Rudolf Dreikurs:*

The Class Council is a 'coming together' of teachers and students in a circle. It should be held regularly, at least once a week. The teacher should be 'in the background' (although also sitting in the circle). The students elect a new spokesperson /leader from time to time who leads the council. There is a class-council-book for students to record their concerns and issues before the meeting and only these are discussed by the council.

If needed the teacher(s) can nudge the talks in certain directions by asking helpful questions. As a rule, it is the responsibility of the children to find the solutions. There is a focus on constructive language. Nobody is shamed or blamed or otherwise humiliated.

If necessary, the teacher(s) can intervene without embarrassing the child who may have said something 'inappropriate'.

To the others: *„What is your opinion?"*
"How do you feel when you hear that?"
„Do you have any ideas as to how you might express that in a different way?"

These are useful questions to stimulate the children's thinking-processes and confidence to express their views. (There is no judgement.)

It takes patience and 'trust in advance' by the teacher(s). It may take a while for the children to dispense with their 'old ways' (put downs) and get used to new positive expressions.

This kind of class-council is a construct which can be performed very well by older children and teenagers. However, in Primary Schools it is better to keep it simple.

In my case I scaled it down because I only saw the children for two hours a week and so used this integrative method for limited periods.

In another group I allowed the children to stick a peg with their name on, onto a self-made 'Emotion-barometer'. We could all see how they felt each day. Following that I told them that we would set up our own group-rules for the morning. This was necessary so that there would be more positive behaviour (self awareness) and they would be better protected from disagreements. I had a pencil and paper in my hands and a talking stick ready for the first round. Mària Kenessey suggested four rounds for the 'class esteem boosting exercise':

Class-council: Boosting Esteem
First round: Encouragement
Each child declares what he / she finds great in the group, what went well this (or last) week, what he / she liked and what progress they had made.

This is **positive tuning in, activating the pleasure centre in the brain.** In this way the group is led away from the mind set of accusations (which would lead to fear, frustration and anger) to good feelings and constructive thinking that creates more possibilities for solutions, happening in a relaxed atmosphere.

Second round: The Wishing Round.
Each child shares what he/she would need to feel better. Nobody is accused of being involved in the non-well-being of others. Nobody is blamed for their feelings and / or expressing their concerns.
Here the children speak openly of situations where they do not feel comfortable in the group. So it may happen that they say something like:
„Dieter is always hitting me!"
Then I would ask:
„What is it that you need to feel safe in this group?"
„He should stop hitting me!"
„Would you like him to be friendly towards you?"
Or
„Would you rather he left you alone?"

I turn the accusation into a wish which the children learn to do quickly as soon as they acknowledge and understand how to use positive communication.
An observation to illustrate this:
There is a great deal of noise in the classroom and one boy starts shouting, then corrects himself in the middle of his sentence: "Don`t be so ... uh ... Can you be more quiet, please?"
Third round: Contributions.
Each child volunteers what he/she could contribute to one of the expressed wishes. The individual issues become less important and are not personal any more. Every child contributes which boosts the self-esteem of every child and the weaker ones grow stronger.

The loud confident children don`t need to interrupt any more because they are constructively occupied in developing the well-being of the group!

Forth round: *Cooperative Activities for Celebration, (without competition)* or munching something together. I often let the children dance to their own music they have brought in so they can get the physical exercise that their bodies need.

A few clear, understandable, well thought out rules, worked out together with the children will be easier to keep.

Example:
The five most important rules in the (music)-class:

1. We take care of ourselves, our class-mates and the instruments.
2. We are friendly, mindful and help each other.
3. We take part and contribute with our own ideas.
4. We listen to each other.
5. We arrive to class on time.

Sometimes we solved problems during break times. Perhaps three of us or a small group as it would have taken up too much time to involve all children and in the lesson.

In my experience these events became faster and easier after starting the class-council. It is amazing how fast children can learn!

Peace-making made easy.

2nd grade. Towards the end of the lesson we play a loud active game to loosen up. Instead of joining in Nadia and Amanda are in a deep discussion. Amanda seems depressed, her face hard as stone. The bell rings for break-time. In the corridor it escalates.
„I see you two are fighting with each other."
They scream and shout and blame each other. I stop them: *„Just a moment!"* I ask the other children to go outdoors and enjoy their break because this was an issue between the two of them and I tell them that Nadia and Amanda will come out as soon as they have made everything clear and have solved their problem. In the meantime Nadia and Amanda calm down a little.
„Can you solve this on your own or do you need my help?"
They want my help. I get two chairs for them and kneel down between them touching their shoulders from time to time while we talk. One of the girls makes a movement. *„You want to say something?"* Amanda begins. Nadia had pushed her. Then they had an argument about their friendship book. The threats went from tearing pages out to demolishing the other`s room and house!
„Now the two of you are very angry at each other."
Pause. Amanda looks sad. I acknowledge it. *„Are you sad?"* „Yes! I find it mean how she treats me!"
„Do you want to say something to this, Nadia?"
„Well, Amanda has been so unfriendly to me and above all she has been mean to me for a long time!"
Amanda bursts into tears: „Yes, because you were my friend when you first came into this class. Then you started playing with the others more and more and I felt pushed out!!!"

I am surprised at how well she can express herself, surprised about the depth of the hurt and glad about the insight I had been granted!
There is much more behind this than the pushing and the book!
I offer empathy.
"This makes you sad, this hurts."
She sobs and nods. Nadia also looks sad and disheartened. *"You are also sad Nadia?"* She nods. *"Amanda, what is your wish? What would you need to feel better? What would both of you need?"* "That she is my friend!" *"Did you hear that Nadia? Do you want that?"* "Yes!" *"Yes. I have the impression that you both like each other, right?"* They nod feeling a little bit embarrassed.

"Well, how can we solve this then and bring back some peace and order? Do you have any ideas? How do you usually make peace?"

Neither of them wants to make the first move. Maybe I am too quick. I wait a little and then I ask if they would like to know what we do in other groups. They nod. *"Well... we have a certain song and it goes like this: "I am sorry 'cause of before on the playground, I am really so sorry ... "*
Suddenly they join in the song, sing with me till the 'Now' and make their peace-making signs, laugh and look really relieved. (They knew this song already from their teacher!) I tell them how pleased I am that my songs make the rounds in the school. Then we go into the playground for the rest of the break in adorable snow which had fallen the night before.

Mario and the grapes

2nd grade pupils enter the play-ground together with the younger children to play with them in the snow (developing relationships) and stay outdoors with them until the lesson starts again. We learn a song whilst building a snow castle together. One girl has a plastic-box containing grapes with her. When we enter the class-room again the box is empty without her having eaten one single grape! Several accusations are flying through the air. We make a circle and I tell them that we shall continue the lesson as soon as we have solved this problem.

Angela says that Mario had eaten all the grapes. He denies it. I ask Angela whether she had seen it, she says no. Inga says that she had seen Mario eat one grape. I look at Mario, and trying humour ask: *„Were you that hungry?"* He smiles relieved and admits: „Yes!" The others protest and say that this is not okay.

"How do you think he should have behaved?" „He should have asked!" „We must tell our class-teacher!"
„What will happen then?" „She will tell him off!"
„Will this bring the grapes back?" They laugh. They are softened up a little bit already, so I tell them that I would prefer to solve it here. Jonas wants to revisit an old story but I don`t allow this: *„I don`t want to hear old stories, they are over!"* Then I suggest that Angela and Mario go to one side to solve their disagreement because it was an issue between them. I ask them if they could manage that and they agree. As they move away they do not look so unhappy. As they come back into the circle they are grinning. I ask if they have 'cleared it up'. Yes, they had. The children wanted to know how they had come to an agreement and Angela bursts out: „I gave him one more chance!"

Pocket-Money

Children should be given pocket-money to train dealing with money. I recommend a weekly small amount from school-age on. They can exercise to save money to fulfil themselves bigger or smaller wishes. My daughter wanted to buy expensive label-clothes, so I gave her the money I thought suitable, and the rest she had to contribute herself.

Important: do not use pocket-money-shortening as 'punishment' or consequence. But certainly let them pay for things they have broken in anger or on purpose.

Sharing, Taking Away

The human brain has no 'compartment' for the idea of 'possession'. So, for children it is extremely difficult to learn the difference between 'mine' and 'yours'. It takes a lot of patience and sympathetic understanding.

Scene:
in the sand-pit:
A father urges his child to give back the shovel it had taken from another child: „This belongs to Benny. Give it back immediately!"
Benny`s mother: „Now lend it to Felix! He wants to have it so much!"
Crying on both sides.
Prevention: Take your own little shovel to share in a case like that. At the same moment one child takes something you give yours to the other and become a **role-model:**

"Look, you can have my shovel."

Sharing should happen voluntarily. When children are forced or persuaded to share there is even more resistance. Every child and human being wants to decide freely for him/herself!
Another possibility when I am quick enough:
„Stop! Just a moment. We always ask:
„Can I have this, please?"
And then you wait to see what the other child says. What did he / she say? No? **'No' is okay.** *Yes, this child does not want to share his / her shovel with you, not yet. You will see, later he / she will be ready to share!"*
(Giving trust in advance.)

The other child is hearing all of this and wants to be included, that`s why he / she maybe willing to give the object later.
I only talk to the child that has been denied the shovel and acknowledge his / her feelings.

„Are you sad? Shall we wait together till Benny is ready? What could you offer him in return? What would you like to play with me in the meantime?"

Give take up time. Don`t comfort feelings away. When the child is crying he / she should be able to finish crying in his / her own time. No pressure. If he / she is angry or in despair we reflect his / her feelings:

„Yes, now you are very, very angry! Yes, this is really awkward! Let it out. Here, on the ground, on this trunk. You know, he is not ready to share yet, this is okay."

With toddlers this action is sufficient. With older children in the play-group age (3) I try this request:

„Can I have this please?"
„Can I please borrow this?"
„I`d love the guitar, do you want the drum instead?"

For more relaxed sharing playtimes at home we can discuss in advance which toys are to share and which are not. They can put those they do not want to share in one box. In another box they put all those toys they are ready to share. We as parents can prepare a box with our 'personal toys' (real children's toys) that we bought for this occasion and that are brought out from time to time when there are visitors, to share.
Of-course we also share them with our own children when they ask.

Set clear limits in a positive way, offering an alternative:
„These are my glasses, they stay on my nose! You can have these (maybe old plastic) sun-glasses."
„This is my computer, I am the only one working on it. You can sit on my lap and press this key for me, then we can look at some pictures together."
„I am the only one who switches the light on and off. ...to turn on the oven etc."
„This machine is for adults only. We can practise how to use this later." (Tell exactly, when.)
„This is my guitar, I turn the pegs but you can pluck / strum the strings and play music with me."
„You can turn the pegs on the ukulele, this is absolutely your job."

"This is Petra`s bicycle, we leave this for her. We can ask her if she will let you ride it some time."
"We let Mrs Miller`s flowers grow. We can touch stroke and smell them though."
"Look, we can pick these flowers in the meadow. We can make a lovely bouquet for the dining table."

Making a Call
(see 'Being quiet' ... 135)

Death

Forest playgroup:
Concerning death.
Through experiencing the four seasons in every year and every weather we not only watch the bursting out of the first birch-leaves or acorn-seedlings but we also experience the passing stages. We observe the changing of dandelions into a multitude of mini flying parachutes (dandelion clocks) in summer, the fading of the colours, the falling and withering of the leaves in autumn. At all times of the year we find dead frogs, birds, butterflies, beetles, mice and moles. For small children meeting death is something quite normal. The child is not or not yet influenced by adult opinions and attitudes and has not developed any taboos.

I have noticed that most children are interested in dead animals, and one or another would tell us of a relative or cat that had recently passed away.

We would always examine a found dead animal. Take them with us, bed them nicely and search for a good place for the funeral. We would even make a cross and put it on top of the small grave mound. One child wanted us to sing a song and so we did. When they asked what would happen I did not explain it away:

„Small animals, tiny little beetles and worms will eat up the body, so they can live. Only the bones will be left in the end."

Children need the truth told in an age appropriate way being mindful to each child's level of comprehension:

„Aunt Rosie died. She does not live anymore."

„Everything turns to earth and goes back to Mother Earth."

„And what about heaven?"

„What do you believe? What do you imagine heaven is?"

It helps to talk about it. I let the children speak.

Fact is: I do not know!

I listen and say that we all have opinions, some are different to ours. It is important that the issue of death is taken seriously and given space when the topic arises.

Mostly, children become very quiet when we talk about it. I think they feel they have been taken seriously and a deep contentment results. After that – it is done with. Death belongs to life and is part of it, even if it is the last stage. Grief belongs in our feelings, it is allowed and has its space.

Maybe you know or find a children`s book where a story is told about someone dying. Check whether it suites your ideas and way of thinking.

Loss can generate anger, not only grief. Take all feelings seriously and allow them to surface.

Sadness, Grief
(also see 'Feelings' … 103,
'Illness' … 116, 'Death' … 170)

Every feeling has its origin and is justified even if the cause sometimes seems to be far from clear.
One client recounts:
„As a child I was sometimes sad and cried `for no reason`. Once it must have been unbearable for my mother because she asked me why I made such a face. I said that I did not know. She slapped me in the face and said: `Now at least you know why you are crying!` "
This mother was not in the least aware of how deeply she hurt and humiliated her child. In early childhood many things are happening that hurt us but we do not remember most of them. When we do 're-member' we are recalling the event and feel it inside ourselves - again. If we call up this pain and embrace it – maybe then the emotional wound can heal.
We cannot protect our children from life, cannot save them from all injury and injustice. Also, we ourselves sometimes hurt our children. However, we can become more aware so that we do not hurt them on purpose or thoughtlessly. Every harsh word, every humiliation leaves traces. Every blow, every spank is harmful even though there is still this old saying: "A little spanking has never done any harm!" How do we know? It is not true. Every verbal or corporal hurt leaves traces and scars.

„Does it hurt a lot?"
„Sometimes I am also sad."
„Right here in the heart, right? Yes, I know this feeling."

"Yes, this hurts a lot, doesn't it! Come, we will bear this together! I am here with you!"
"Yes, cry, let it all out!"
"Let the tears flow. Afterwards you will feel better!"
"Would you like to sit beside me?"
"Would you like me to hold you? (Embrace you? Give you a hug?)"

Admit and express your own pain and sadness:
"Yes, I am sad. But this is alright."
"Yes, grownups cry sometimes as well."
"I do not feel so well. I am going to take a break and lie down for half an hour."

Picture from the integrative Parent-training Switzerland
„Could you give him something for my nerves?"

Fits of Anger and Tantrums
The so-called 'Tantrum-phase'

It is a fact: the term 'tantrum-phase' is not found in the 'Encyclopaedia of Parenting Errors' – because this phase does not exist.

A colleague of mine who works in Therapeutic, Education and Healing said to me: „It should be called `autonomy-phase` and it should last until we are ninety!"

In a parent training session I asked the parents present to name terms that they associated with the word 'tantrum'. Before that I asked if there were any parents whose child never had a tantrum. No, they all knew that.

„I can assure you: your children are healthy!", was my answer.

So what are the signs of a tantrum?

Here are some of the answers from the parents that might sound familiar to you:

"Don`t want!"
„Want this! Want that!"
Even: „I want a different daddy!"
„No!" (I asked: who did she / he get this from?)
„You are mean!"
„If you don`t ... then ...!"

Anger, rage, aggression, screaming, frustration, stress at being completely overwhelmed, not being able to let it go.

Empty threats.

Corporal violence, injuries.

Helplessness, outrage.

Insignificance.
Fights, power-struggles, mainly in public.
Flight

Yes, sometimes we just want to run away – and so do the children!

Where does this come from so suddenly?
Before tantrums the child has been the sweetest darling! For a whole year or two. Then this completely strange new behaviour suddenly occurs!
I do not recognise my child anymore and /or even myself!
The harmony of the family now is threatened. There is seemingly constant fighting and arguing and at the most unsuitable times!
Just as this behaviour arrived it goes – or does not! That is why this time is often called a 'phase', even in trainings and studies. It goes together with the ...

... basic needs of children
In the first year of its life the baby is primarily fully cared for (hopefully!). It gets everything it needs, suffers only from little frustrations, develops its capabilities, and has (when it is lucky) built up a positive emotional relationship with its relations. In this way the child will have achieved a general feeling of **safety and trust.**
But then, when one year old, it begins to stand up and walk. Now he or she can reach everything that is within reach and this is what he / she really wants!
It is like a big force from inside, an urge, a yearning and is part of growing up: to explore, taste, feel, touch, discover, try – every thing! His / her main goals are the

expanding of the horizon and the conquering of the surroundings.
Following this urge the child is suddenly confronted with the limits of the adults who say „No!" or „Be careful, this is dangerous!" „Don`t touch! Let go! You are not allowed to ... Stop this immediately!" etc. In the mind of the child the once protecting grownups have turned into monstrous enemies that the child is helplessly exposed to. It does not understand the world anymore!

The **despair of the child** is expressed by aggression: it is screaming, stomping, kicking, hollering. When the adults punish this behaviour, when they scold him / her, the vicious cycle is completed and turns again.

How to cope with these fits? How to correct this?
Offer the toddler child-adapted surroundings where he / she can have interesting and exciting experiences that feed the hunger for exploration. Rearrange your bookshelves, put things higher up, out of reach.

Set clear limits in which the child can move freely. Defend your limits friendly and consequently, preferably **without talking or explaining too much**. Just act, put the child where it can play. Try not to limit the experiences. Join in and be amazed by their play. Have an extra handbag / drawer containing harmless things to be emptied out. (Tissues to be torn to pieces, wooden spoons, sauce pans, a whisk to make music and experiment).

Communication: the 'Yes-language'
(instead of the continual 'No' which releases aggressions) with children from about (2) to (4):

"Yes, I know you would like to have an ice-cream now. Today we have already had one. Tomorrow we may have another one. I am looking forward to playing with you in the garden now."

"Yes, I know you don`t like the seat belt. Here in the car / in the bus / in the aeroplane we do what we have read about. Do you remember in the book? The pilot is also strapped in. Daddy fixes his belt. Also mummy. And you too, now we are all strapped in and safe."

"Yes, this is a very nice, delicate porcelain figure. It goes up on the shelf to sleep there."

Redirecting (offering an option):

"We can use the plastic jug to scoop water."
"Yes, I know you like flowers. These here we let grow, you can stroke and smell them though."

Use the magic phase:
Everything is alive and has a personality.

"The dummy is now in the dummy playgroup. You can have it this evening."
"The shoes we can park here, look, like a row of cars in the car park."

Allow and name the feelings:
"Yes, now you are sad (angry)."

Instead of forbidding something describe what you want to see, tell the children what you want them to do, using 'we-language':

„We do it like this..."
(Live it. Children learn through watching our behavior. We are role models.)
Stay calm, talk less but act if there is danger. Do not explain everything (this makes them tired, they do not listen anymore.)
Like a rock in the breakers:
Stay friendly (if possible) when they are like roaring storms around you. Take your time.

The less we frustrate and threaten the child and the more we encourage and strengthen them the simpler parenting becomes!

How to Neglect Misbehaviour

If possible, **neglect behaviour you do not like**:
Ayla (2) is chewing on coloured pencils at the table, looking provocatively at her father. Up to now he has always scolded her because he was worried for her. As this did not bring about any desired results he tried to ignore her behaviour. He only looked at her (curious as to what might happen this time!). Again she is chewing the pencils, looking at her father, looking at the pencils, making a face and throwing the pencils away. They are not tasty! So now it is no longer an issue. Nobody is reacting!
When we take 'our sails out of their wind', annoying behaviour is no longer worthwhile. Afterwards, this father starts to talk to Ayla, dedicating himself to her and giving her his complete attention. He does not mention the pencils or the behaviour.
Give attention when you see the desired conduct. Talk, show you are interested, share, include the child and

so provide the basis for more self-assurance, self-confidence and self-esteem through the feeling of belonging together by being together.

We often interfere when it is not necessary. What if we let the child be?

A boy is scooping a bucket full of sand and is emptying it over his own head. I am silently observing, curious as to what will happen. He shakes himself. He repeats it. And after that he plays something different. Now he knows how it feels - and that is that!

Had I interfered I would have deprived him of this experience. Had he emptied the pail over another head I would have come and asked the other child how this felt for him / her. Attend to this child, not to the one who emptied the bucket.

"How is it for you?"

"You don't like it? Would you like to tell him to stop?"

"You know that when we say STOP the other one has to stop? You practice this in circle time don`t you?"

"Would you like us to help you get clean?"

And to the other child:

"You can help me shake the sand out of his / her clothes. Then he / she will feel fine again."

See how the elder sister is copying the younger brother

The Role Model

We are role models when we act, speak and behave as we would like our children to behave.

„In our family we do it like this ..."

„I put my shoes side by side like the cars in the car park."

If I have been loud I apologise:

„I am sorry, it was not my intention to shout at you. It is neither good for you or me."

„Could you help me and remind me when I get too loud? I would like to keep my promises!"

„Or when I am getting mad at you could you ask: Are you going to be angry now, mum? (dad?). This would help me a lot!"

I have read somewhere: „Actually we don`t need to parent our children - they copy us anyway!"

And of-course they copy each other.

Khaleesi is joyfully jumping and running on a mattress – little Aaliyah and Coco follow behind! What fun!

Fighting Back, Defending (Yourself)

An often used and very discouraging sentence:
„You have to defend yourself / hit back!"
At the same time we teach our children to be peace loving. So what do you do? How can we encourage and support them?
The answer: give them responsibility. Or better: give them back their own responsibility (that we had taken away from them)

„Yes, this is awkward."
„What could you do?"
„What would you like to do? / prefer?"
„How should they behave?"
"How would it be more comfortable / pleasant for you?" „What do you think you could say to them?"

My daughter was persistently persecuted by our neighbour`s son. She was running away from him and coming to me, complaining.

One solution worked very well as in my playgroups and music-lessons (because the truth of the situation was revealed): interpret the behaviour and direct it in a positive direction.
So I said:
„Most probably he finds you interesting, but he does not know how to show it!"

The assailant also heard this and consequently his conduct changed and created a new situation. Also my daughter felt rather flattered. It worked. He left her in peace.

Changing Nappies

A mother asks her young son Simon: „Shall we change your nappy now?" Of-course Simon does not want this. She persuades and coaxes him. She really wants to change his nappy! Her husband considers this and tells her that this was not a real question. She should tell the child what she wants, not ask him.

I confirm this and advise her to let Simon choose the place. (Offer two choices.) Create a joyful atmosphere with body-games, rhymes, little songs so both can look forward to the changing. She could also say and play 'changing wheels' instead of 'changing nappies'.

"The big red car is in the garage and we are going to change the wheels now!"

Another favourite I used with my children:

„Now the big bear starts at the foot of the mountain (feet), smells at the berries on the bush (toes), eats some of them (munching at the toes), then he slowly climbs up the hill to the rocks over the knees, passes a big river (thighs), ah, here is the fountain, your penis (your vagina) and behind the bear found a big, soft cushion, that is your bottom! ..."

By naming all the body parts the child learns to know and feel his / her body. Also name the sexual organs correctly.

There can also be some tickling, but be careful not to overdo it. The child cannot defend itself and although laughing, might not want it anymore! Be mindful and sensitive to this.

Resistance

Children who hear, oh so many! 'Nos', 'Don'ts' and demands can develop incredible resistance. This is their healthy reaction to our parenting. Every human being wants to be his / her own boss and experiences frustration, anger, grief and aggression when they receive too many demands or reprimands.
How can we remedy this?

„You know, suddenly I've realised that you have grown up so much! From now on you can take some responsibilities and decide about certain things yourself." (Giving back 'self-responsibility').
„It goes without saying that you can ask me any time you need help, and then we can discuss it. I do appreciate it when you tell me how you come to your decisions."
„I'm so proud of you!"

„From now on it get's better!"

„You can tell me later how you came to that decision. There is no hurry."

„We rearrange getting up. You can set this alarm clock for yourself as from tomorrow."

„You can choose for yourself what you want to have for breakfast. I shall put everything on the table for quickness."

„During the week I will clear the table. At the weekend you can do this in turns. Who wants to start?"

„You can buy your own clothes. You can have (a certain amount) at your disposal. Any extra you may need you can supplement from your pocket money."

„There are jobs that have to be done by everyone, and others where you can earn money. We can discuss these in detail in the family meeting (family-council)."

„Yes, it is important that you think about things and decide for yourself. I trust you! – Well at least I can try!"

And the hardest sentence ever in my opinion
(can also only be thought by yourself):

"Yes, I know I have to let you go sooner or later.
You have to discover the world by yourself!"

Brushing Teeth

We can sing about beautiful, white, shiny, healthy teeth. This kind of celebration reaches the self-rewarding-centre in the brain. (Endorphins!)
As a consequence the children feel good, experience enjoyment, happiness and want more of it!
Then we get what we want ... simply, easily and everyone benefits i.e.: children opening their mouths long enough and staying interested in the otherwise boring activity of cleaning their teeth.

A small piece of advice: threatening is harmful and destructive to our children. It puts an end to the joy of caring for their teeth. That is why we discard the stories of fearful little devils and other monsters in their mouths and concentrate on what is desired. We can practise with them until they can do it by themselves. After that: do not correct them. Your trust in them makes them proud!

An integrative positive outcome (using 'friendly consequence'):

If the child does not want to brush his / her teeth we cut out all sweets for the next day (staying friendly!):

„Today we are only eating fruits and vegetables so you will not need to brush your teeth. No, sorry, there is no chocolate today, no, also no biscuits, they contain sugar. I want your teeth to stay nice and white and that you won`t have pain."
Mentioning 'painful tooth decay' would be frightening. If the child is asking what might happen I can tell.

"Yes, as soon as you want to brush your teeth again you can eat sweets and cake again."
One mother tells us how she tried this out successfully:
„As my son refused to brush his teeth once again I simply said: `Okay, then you don`t have to brush your teeth.` **I did not mention the sweets or any consequences. (This was important! So he could not argue!)** The next day when all the other children had ice cream he did not get one. He had a huge tantrum but I stayed calm and resolute. He screamed and raged for an hour but I did not give in. I bore it and did not give him one little sweet. At the same time I stayed astonishingly calm, understanding and friendly.
In the evening he wanted to brush his teeth! From that time on it has never been a problem. Once we were on a holiday and I was tired from a long hike and groaning that I had to brush my teeth on top of everything! He said: `Mum, you'd better brush your teeth right now otherwise you can`t eat sweets tomorrow!`"

To bear the torrent produces miracles!
Being like a rock in the water.

Please note: after sour food you have to wait about thirty minutes before cleaning teeth as the acid softens the enamel. It is better to swill the mouth with water or Xylitol. Sweeten foods with Xylitol or Stevia powder as a healthy alternative which also strengthens the teeth.

Here is one of my teeth brushing songs that I composed:
"Let`s brush your teeth, brush your teeth,
brush your little teeth!
Up and down ....
Left and right ....

Look, how they are shining bright!
Let`s brush your teeth, brush your teeth,
yes, it is great fun!"

One mother invented stories that continued every evening. The main character was her daughter: a princess who is cleaning the horses' stable with a golden tooth-brush that she had picked from a golden tree in her magic garden. She lovingly brushes her horses and cats and so on. With a boy it could be a garage or even an aeroplane hangar. The mechanic is checking all the screws, cleans the motor etc. Use the child's 'magic stage' in their development to mutual benefit !

„What is parked in your garage today? A Bentley? Oh, then we have to clean and brush every corner completely and carefully!"
„A tractor? Okay, then let`s start! There is much work to do! I am up for this!"

The tooth brush is gentle and curious:

„I am coming for a visit. Knock, knock, may I enter? I look into every corner: Wow, this is great in here! Really clean, white, snug and warm! You take good care of my furniture!"

„The clean team is here and brushes away the last little pieces! Hurray!"

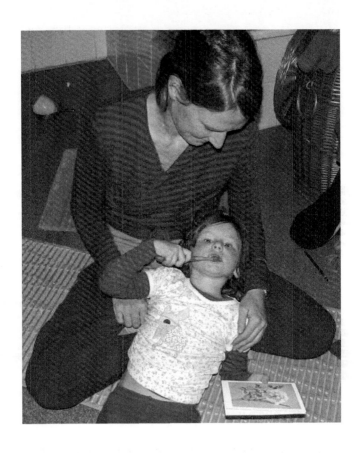

Take time. Bring comfort, closeness
and careful attention to the teeth brushing.
This makes it a wonderful socio-positive experience
that strengthens your relationship
and boosts your child's self-esteem
through happiness and intimacy.

(Loreena and her mother)

Listening
(also see 'Being quiet' ... 135)

Try to just listen. Just as you wished when a child or maybe still wish. Take time and give one-hundred percent attention. Do not make assumptions. Ask. Ask caring questions about their feelings and take all responses seriously.

When children do not listen it may be because the adults are talking too much, repeat themselves, admonish them too often and give explanations that are too long (boring). Children get the feeling that they are thought of as stupid, feel misunderstood, and so their resistance increases.

Harmful sentences: „Why don`t you ever listen!"
„I told you a hundred times!" (Yes, that`s why!)

More constructive:

„You did not understand / hear this? I am sorry, next time I will make sure and check that you have understood."

„I probably did not express myself clearly enough."

„What would help you to keep our rules better?"

„What could help you to remember next time?"

If you plan to explain less to your children in future, discuss it first with them:
„I have noticed that I over explained, repeated myself and kept reminding you." (I am talking in the past tense as if it were over already. This helps to leave this habit.

If you talk in the present tense you bring it with you and take it into the future. Just cut it.)

"You are older now and are able to take responsibility for yourself. That is why I will try not to talk so much in future. And if I do, please remind me! That would help me to keep my promise."

Arriving late

Throw away those old sentences that you have been using up to now and surprise your children with something completely new. In a genuine way without any sarcasm which is poison in any relationship!

„Good, great that you are here."
„We have eaten already but you are lucky: there is still something left!"
„We have reserved a seat for you."
„What a pity you have just missed the joke. Would you like to tell one tomorrow at the beginning of the lesson?"

„How many times would you like to come late?"

„We normally play a game before we start. It would be great if everyone was here together." (Invitation, **welcome to all**, so the focus child feels included but not identified.)

Or just go ahead with the activity without mentioning it, hopefully awakening a desire to come and join in on time next time:

"Oh, you're lucky, the game is not over yet! You can still play till the end! "

You might consider possible reasons for the lateness:
People (not only children) who arrive late might feel insecure, not really eager to join in or just bored. Most of the time they then get extra attention (often negative). Not noticing too much, just nodding without interrupting one`s speech or using a welcoming 'matter of fact' sentence could help to prevent this habit.

And so here, towards the end of this book an additional place to dump more of those taboo-words or sentences that you have discovered to be harmful. Or at least not useful in your relationships:

These are the ones that reach the 'fear-centre' in the brain. They contain the threats that make children more insecure. They intimidate and are untruths which tend to stick. They only show our own dissatisfaction and distress. They are delivered as reproaches that do harm, are hurtful and upset your relationship. They are shaming, blaming, excluding, humiliating, and discouraging.

never
must / have to
should
always
finally
and again!
not even
a hundred times
good, bad

can`t you at least ...
for once
You are late again!
Where have you been!
... for so long!
I told you!
See?
Get a move on!
(sarcastically) Take your time!
Now this is the last time!
I shall never again take you to .
I warn you!
You'll put me in my grave!
Come here immediately!
Otherwise ...!
You never obey!
Of-course any rude names
or swear-words like bitch, pig,
clown, fool, etc. (You know, which hurt ys. as a child!)
You are so silly, untidy, lazy, untidy, sloppy, beastly,
nasty, troublesome! ...etc.
Now we have to leave, OKAY? (Why do you ask?)

> My / our own Taboo-words and sentences, that I dump here:
> ....
> ....
> ....
> ....
> ....
> ....
> ....
> ....
> ....
> ....

And now some more Golden Sentences containing miracle-words:

Today we are just great and we are getting better day by day.
We always support each other.
I am so glad you are you!
Can you do that on your own or do you need help?
All of us have jobs in our group / family.
Yes, I know.
Life is not fair.

In our family we help each other.
We listen to each other.
In our family / kindergarten we speak kindly to each other.
As soon as you have washed your hands you can come for lunch.
Thank Goodness it is not so bad!
Does not matter, this can happen to anyone.

What do children need and what makes living together with children easier and more pleasant?:

Learn from mistakes:
„*Mistakes are our friends. From them we learn.*"
Unconditional acceptance:
„*I love you exactly as you are.*"
Let them take their own responsibility:
„*In my play-group the children can do this by themselves.*" (*But you can help each other.*)

Encouragement:
"You will see, next week this will go much better!"

Friendly (kind but firm) consequences:
*"I am sorry, this stick goes on a holiday.
Tomorrow you can practise again.
What will you do with the stick then?
You have an idea?"*
*"What a shame! The sausages are all eaten.
But there are some potatoes left."*
"How can you fix that? Do you have a suggestion?"

Allow feelings to flow:
"Yes cry, let it all out, it will do you good."
"Your joy is so beautiful to see!"

Yes-language and We-language:
"At grandma`s we can play on the carpet. At home you can jump on the sofa."

Clear limits:
"Ouch, this hurts. We are kind to each other."
"We treat each other with kindness / with respect!"

Seek out opinion / look closer:
"What do you think? Is this jacket warm enough for today?" *"Do we have enough food for the picnic or shall we pack some more?"*

Safety:
"We take care of each other."
"I am there if you need me."
Being a role model:
"When I am angry I hit the cushion."

Trust in advance:
„I am absolutely sure you will be able to do it!"

Giving choice:
*„What would you like to do first?
Brush your teeth or shower?"*

And four „f" – reminders:
freedom, free will, firmness and friendliness

Plus:
affection, warmth, closeness, care and attention, joy, fun, play, movement, nature and space.

The basic belief of the integrative teaching method is unconditional acceptance.

Myself with 2 1/2

Anahita with Loreena

What does 'integrative parenting' mean?

It is the culmination and development of all the teaching, psychological, neurological exchange of ideas together with all the family therapeutic knowledge known to date (2017) that support the holistic growth of the child.

Ideas collated and made new by Mària Kenessey at her own institute IfIPP.
(Institute for Integrative Psychology and Pedagogics)
To give you some names:
Friedrich Fröbel, J. H. Pestalozzi (heart, hand and brain)
Maria Montessori (Neuropsychology)
Alfred Adler (Psychology of the individual)
Milton Erickson, Gerald Hüther (Brain research).

Integrative Parenting supports the holistic fostering of the child. The transmitted values of this method are in accordance with the UN-Human rights and the Declaration of the Rights of Children UNICEF. They include the basic rights of democracy. What does this actually mean?
Integrative Parenting is resource based and encouraging. We set clear limits and see that the rules that we agree together are being kept.
There are logical, natural, gentle consequences. (No scolding or other punishments).
Resource-oriented means:
we look for and reinforce the good in the child.
We notice the desired behavior, do not react to misbehavior; and reprimanding is dispensed with.

The Leading Idea of the Kenessey-Method

The integrative method ...

1. Strengthens the self-esteem of the child.
2. Enhances the feeling of belonging.
3. Builds up an equal relationship with children.
4. Supports responsibility and the ability to make decisions.
5. Strengthens the love of themselves, of others and of nature.
6. Points to the miracles of creation.
7. Shows a positive sight of the world.
8. Gives safety and reduces children's fears.
9. With its philosophy and practice this method supports the ability to solve conflicts and strengthens the readiness to repair and make peace.
10. Supports parents in education and parenting.
11. Supports the individuality of every child and avoids the development of rivalry and power-games.
12. Is friendly, clear, constructive, resource based and emphasises the good in all.

The integrative method is based on the basic rights of democracy.

The integrative method includes the children`s rights of UNICEF:

Children Have the Right to Survive and Develop to the Fullest

Children Have the Right to Express Themselves

Children Have the Right to Appropriate Information

Children Have the Right to Freedom of Conscience

Children Have the Right to Freedom of Thought

Children Have the Right to Privacy

Children Have the Right to a Loving and Caring Family

Children Have the Right to an Education

Children Have the Right to Play

Children Have the Right to Protection from Hazardous Work

Children Have the Right to a Drug Free World

Children Have the Right to Protection from Sexual Abuse

Children Have the Right to Protection from Land mines

Children Have the Right to Protection in Times of War

So ... instead of finishing with an epilogue I will let the pictures speak for themselves.

Title: „The Coronation Finale!"

When the grown-ups are humorous and creative ...

... the children can also play for themselves
(most of the times ...)

Or the other way round: when the children got enough hundred percent caring attention (as you can see, they have got their hair done as well) afterwards they can play alone and the adults have time for each other. (What you do then it`s up to you!)

Also animals are a wonderful company for our children, of-course!

Anahita Huber-Sprügl
Biography

1956: Born in Graz, Austria. We are ten siblings, I am the oldest from six. (There are four older half-brothers and sisters.)

1975: Finished schooling after which I emigrated to South Africa.

1977 Zürich: Raised a family. One daughter, two sons.

From 2000/01: Worked as graduate music teacher and 'integrative' teacher.

2001 to 2008: Studied at the IfIPP (Institute for Integrative Psychology and Pedagogy) with Màrìa Kenessey in Zürich. Training in: Integrative Psychology and Pedagogy, Parent-coaching, Group Leading, Parent Training, Playgroup Supervision, Couple and Family Therapy.

Wakonda Bern: Pedagogy of Outdoor Activities.

2005 - 2009: Started a business offering my own courses.

2010, 2011 and 2017: Voluntary work in an International Kindergarten in India and in a preschool in Sri Lanka.

From 2008-2011: Travelling with partner Deva Abhiyana Freitag in Switzerland, Europe and Asia. Starting to write and publish books.

2012: Settled down in the Kanton Bern. The beginnings of „immerleichter" (which means more and more easy).

What I offer:
Parenting training, Coaching and Supervision

Contact and information:
immerleichter@gmail.com
www.immerleichter.ch

I look forward to your feedback, suggestions, thoughts for additions and evaluations. Naturally I hope that this book will become a well-used reference book for you!

Anahita at the Team-Coaching Jan.2017
in the international Kindergarten in Patnem Goa, India

Integrative pedagogy books by Anahita Huber (German only):

Die integrative Erziehung im Vorschulalter
Theorie und Praxis
Waldkinderkrippe, Musikalische Frühförderung, Musik- und Naturspielgruppe

BoD-Verlag, 280 pages
ISBN 978-3-8482-0925-5

„I want to thank you most heartily for all the wonderful advice in this book. It has helped me a lot!" A mother

Die integrative Pädagogik in der Musikalischen Grundschule
Konstruktiver Umgang mit Konflikten
Theorie und Praxis, Beispiele aus dem Unterricht (1. – 3. Klasse)

BoD-Verlag, 284 Seiten /
ISBN 978-3-7322-3468-4

„The book is very good! I am enthusiastic about it!" Mària Kenessey

Big, big thanks
- to my partner **Deva Abhiyana Freitag** who spent many hours to prepare the pictures so carefully. And for the computer-maintenance also. Without you I would have been at a total loss!

Thanks to Susan Roszkowiak for proof-reading this whole script with sharp eyes and a pedagogic heart for free – your work is so precious and absolutely indispensable! Without you – no way of publishing this book!

Thanks to Maja from the campsite who spontaneously donated money for this project so I did not have to worry about costs too much!

Thanks to all of those who contributed these lovely pictures of their kids and let me publish them! Pratibha and Kareem with Khaleesi cominghome.ch; Yasha with Aaliyah; Tanja, Lathu with Bhasu and Dev and their friends; Elisa with Adil; Silvia, Nina, Mohini, Stephie and Valentin with kids; Simone with Matteo; Ashankit, Isabel with Coco; Doris, Tom with Matteo, and Yvonne and Jürgen with Loreena and Nepomuk. A big hug to all of you!

Thank you all of you for your interest,
ideas, requests and feedbacks.
Without your wishing
this book might not have been born.

I wish all of you a lot of joy and fun with your children,
good success, growth of your knowledge and feeling
in the frame of your possibilities
which may constantly open and widen –
and huge patience when practising!

Be patient especially with yourself!

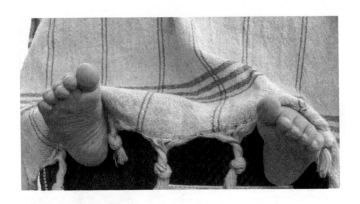

**Thanks to all children, those lovely creatures,
through which we can learn so much!**

**Thank you for your joy, your anger,
your sadness, your happiness,
for your BEING
just
yourself
!**

© 2017
Herstellung und Verlag
BoD - Books on Demand, Norderstedt
ISBN 9 783746 0 16207